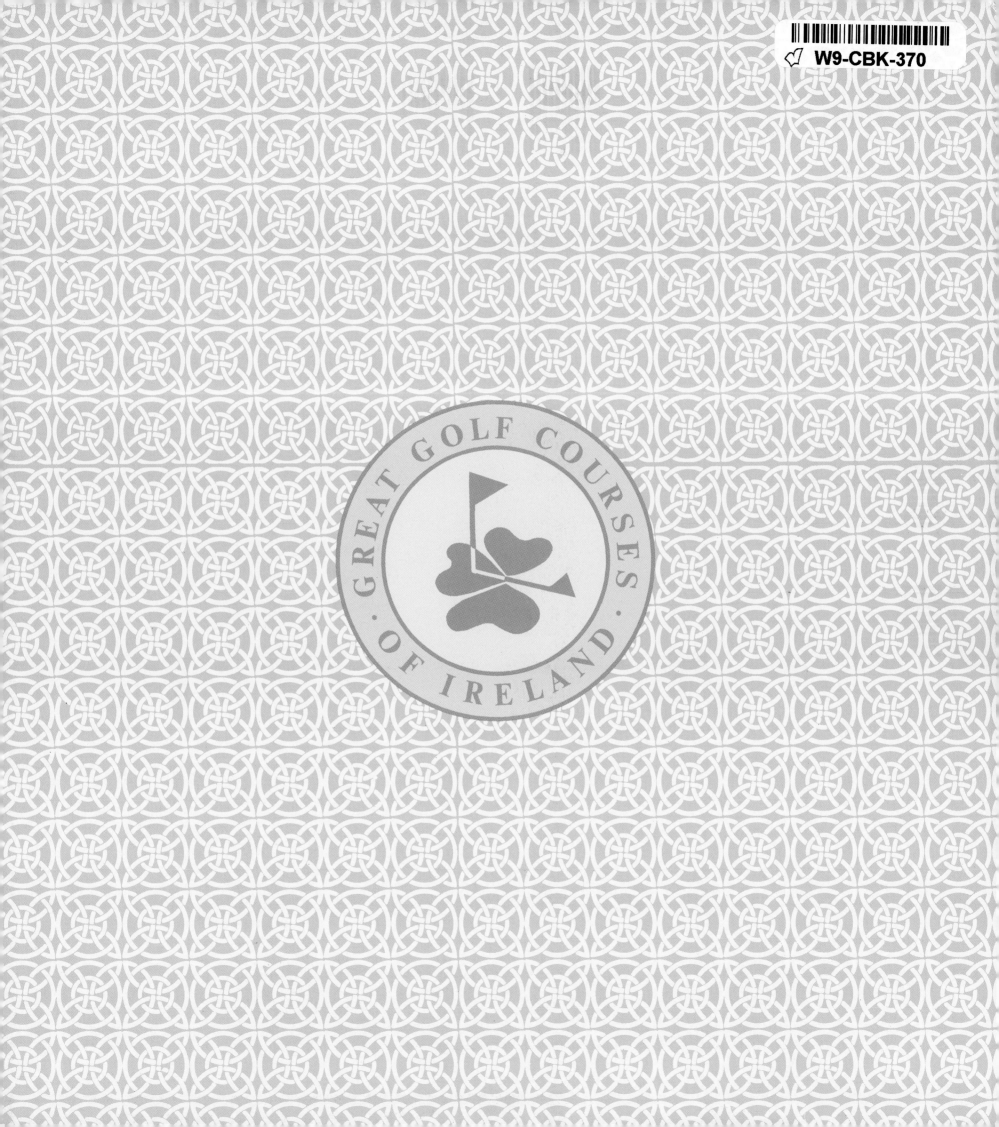

GREAT GOLF COURSES · OF IRELAND ·

DESIGNED BY
PHILIP CLUCAS

PHOTOGRAPHY BY
NEIL SUTHERLAND

ACKNOWLEDGEMENT
The publishers would like to thank all the featured
golf clubs and their staff for the invaluable
assistance provided during the preparation of
this book.

Published in Ireland by Gill & Macmillan Ltd
Hume Avenue, Park West, Dublin 12
with associated companies throughout the world.
www.gillmacmillan.ie

CLB 5149
Originally published by Quadrillion Publishing Ltd, 1999
copyright © Salamander Books Limited, 2001
A member of the Chrysalis Group plc

Printed in Hong Kong
ISBN 0 7171 2875 X

GREAT GOLF COURSES OF IRELAND

GREAT GOLF COURSES OF IRELAND

John Redmond

Gill & Macmillan

CONTENTS

Royal County Down Golf Club

FOREWORD

One of the delightful aspects of life on the professional golf circuit is the opportunity it affords to travel the world and play on some of the finest golf courses. In Europe one day, America the next, with Japan, Australia and other far-flung parts also being visited throughout the golfing year, there is little time for boredom.

As fascinating as the contrasts between these diverse lands and their peoples is the difference in golfing cultures, the courses and their designs. Being deeply interested in course architecture, I find it all totally absorbing and fulfilling, especially as this is an aspect of the game that I would like to pursue in the future.

Invariably a point of conversation, if not argument, among golfers is the type of course and the locations they most enjoy playing. Personally, I do not believe you can have a definitive listing of the finest locations, for while this would take into account the traditions and atmosphere of the leading clubs and courses, it would inevitably be coloured by the successes or failures that one had experienced there. That is how it should be.

Beautifully sited, Ireland's superb golf courses rank among the finest in the world, and the essence of their virtues is captured in this splendid volume, with which I am pleased to be associated. Enjoy it.

Ronan Rafferty

1

BALLYBUNION GOLF CLUB

~ OLD COURSE ~ YARDS: 6,540 ~ PAR: 72 ~

An American golfing aficionado thought so much of Ballybunion Golf Club that on his death-bed he ordered his body to be flown from Los Angeles for burial in the graveyard beside the first tee of the famous Old Course. That last request underlines the captivating spell cast over all those blessed with the fulfilment of having made the pilgrimage to one of the world's greatest links.

The legendary Majors champion Tom Watson, and the renowned course architect Robert Trent Jones, are prominent among

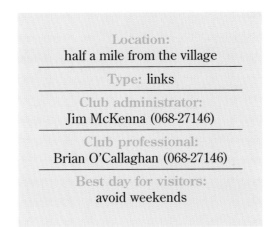

Location:
half a mile from the village

Type: links

Club administrator:
Jim McKenna (068-27146)

Club professional:
Brian O'Callaghan (068-27146)

Best day for visitors:
avoid weekends

the many admirers. 'Playing Ballybunion is similar in many respects to playing Cypress Point in America and I like that style of golf,' says Watson. 'There appear to be no man-made influences and Ballybunion is a course on which many golf architects should live and play before they build golf courses,' adds the giant of golf, who many times practised at his most-loved Irish course before winning some of his five British Open titles.

It was also love at first sight for Trent Jones, the doyen of modern-day designers. 'This is the most natural golf course terrain I have encountered ... I will build you a great course, one of my best,' he exclaimed when the club hired a helicopter to give the man who has had a greater impact than anyone else on golf course architecture since World War II an aerial view of the adjoining site proposed for the New Course.

The upshot is that Ballybunion today is now a world-renowned golf complex of 36 of the finest links land holes you will encounter in any one place.

The Old Course and the New combine in a mighty challenge, and while the Old is a permanent fixture on the recognised lists of Great Golf Courses of the World, it is the contention of club professional Ted Higgins

1 *The haunting opening site by the first tee and 16th green.*
'Ballybunion has a lot of concepts that I might use in my future designs,' said Jack Nicklaus of the famed Old Course – (2) the 17th green.

that the New will, in time, enjoy the same status.

The common theme is the shared glory of being situated in such a wonderful, seemingly unending stretch of natural, tumbling duneland sweeping along the golden sandy shore of the Atlantic Ocean and by the mouth of the River Shannon.

Ballybunion's geographically pictur-esque location as a lively holiday town comes at a price to golf. The exposed courses are constantly at war with the waves. Each year, thousands of pounds must be spent in an unremitting battle to bolster the shoreline.

The harrowing plight of such heritage

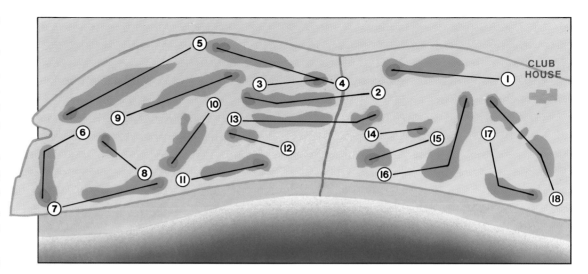

BALLYBUNION GOLF CLUB — Old Course		All measurements in yards.										Competition										Date		
BLUE TEES	SSS 72	392	445	220	498	508	364	423	153	454	3457	359	449	192	484	131	216	490	385	379	3085	3457	6542
WHITE TEES	SSS 70	366	394	211	490	489	344	400	134	430	3258	336	400	179	480	125	207	482	368	366	2943	3258	6201
GREEN TEES	SSS 68	329	379	185	483	476	319	386	116	411	3084	312	384	166	477	118	197	472	350	358	2881	3084	5965
MEN'S PAR		4	4	3	5	5	4	4	3	4	36	4	4	3	5	3	3	5	4	4	35	36	71
INDEX		9	1	11	15	13	7	5	17	3		10	2	16	8	18	4	14	12	6			
A.																							
B.																							
± PTS.																							
HOLE	H'cap	1	2	3	4	5	6	7	8	9	Out	10	11	12	13	14	15	16	17	18	In	Out	Tot.

1 *Classic example of Ballybunion's unique setting.*

being endangered captured the hearts of well-wishers from far beyond Kerry and Ireland in 1977. A particularly bad winter storm that year wreaked havoc with fairways and greens, and a 'Friends of Ballybunion' campaign was launched. The spirited fight against the problems of coastal erosion brought a response sufficient to check the crisis by the placement on the beach of sea-gabions (large boulders encased in wire mesh), designed to decrease the effect of the crashing waves, though not to solve the problem. It is ongoing.

That the defiant members of Bally-bunion are accustomed to a challenge is rooted in their history. While the formation of the first club can be traced to 1891, it seems that interest flamed but then faded, and it was not until 1906 that the club was revived.

Inspiration came from a returned Indian army officer, Colonel Bartholomew, who invited his associate, Lionel Hewson, a golfing scribe, to lay out a nine-hole course.

The club has since prospered, for once the extension to 18 holes was completed in 1927 (with Tom Simpson, the noted British architect, later making some minor adjustments), the reputation of Ballybunion quickly spread as the Irish Women's and Men's Championship, and later the Irish Professional Championship, were staged. Word of mouth did the rest.

There can hardly be a golfing shrine where nature was a greater collaborator than at both the Ballybunion courses. God-given terrain is how Trent Jones attributes the success of the 328-yards par-four 10th, and the spectacular siting for the green at the 387-yards par-four 13th, on his beloved New course. He might have passed similar judgment on the strength of the par fives, a collection of the best to be played anywhere in the world.

When Watson states that 'Ballybunion offers some of the finest and most demanding shots into the greens of any course,' he surely underlines the nature of the 8th hole of only 155 yards (one of five par threes), or the much-acclaimed, and his personal favourite, 446-yards par-four 11th, perched right on the seaside clifftop, and tumbling down through the dunes like a staircase.

What of the phenomenon of Ballybunion's desert? Straddling the 18th fairway, it is a stretch of sand so vast that it is known as the 'Sahara'. The hazard consists of a curious mixture of sand, shells, ashes, stones and bones, the relics dating back over 5,000 years to Mesolithic times.

Beware the vision of Killsaheen! The rare sight appears through the haze of the shimmering Atlantic and consists of an arch or bridge with people walking about, as if at a fair, while in one place close to the arch can be seen an old woman sitting down near a cart or table, evidently selling her wares. Whilst it is a unique privilege to see the vision, it may not altogether be a welcome one, as tradition holds that those who see it will die within seven years!

2 'Friends of Ballybunion' world-wide came to the rescue in 1977 in a fund-raising gesture to fight against coastal erosion. Sea 'gabion' wire baskets, layered with stones, were laid to defuse the in-rushing Atlantic rollers.
3 Relics of a bygone age – the canvas bag and hickory clubs, which belonged to one-time Ireland rugby football international John Macauley, Ballybunion club president 1916-57, were purchased at auction by club professional Ted Higgins.
4 Hole 1 on the New Course.

BELVOIR PARK GOLF CLUB

~ *YARDS: 6,501 ~ PAR: 71* ~

One of the most endearing features of golf in Belfast is that, while so many clubs are located close to the tumult of the city, in the playing of them the golfer is well insulated from its bustle, and the lovely Belvoir (pronounced Beaver) Park, just outside the south city boundary, perfectly illustrates the point.

Its immediate impact is one of peace and tranquillity in a setting of rolling parkland and amid some of the finest specimens of mature timber. Caring consideration in respect of foliage has always been high on the club agenda. You'll see and appreciate why.

Some of the trees on the picturesque course are said to be over 150 years old, and standing on the front porch of the elevated clubhouse (from which it is possible to view virtually every hole), it is easy to picture the scene back in 1927 when the architect Harry Colt supervised the horse-drawn plough and carts, and the teams of work-men, as the course was fashioned from one of the most beautiful pieces of property in the suburbs of Belfast.

The extensive sweep of scenery embraces the Black Mountains, Cavehill, the quaint old village of Newtownbreda and, perhaps, just a glimpse of the much-chronicled Harland and Wolff Shipyards, builders of the ill-fated *Titanic*.

In all, 170 or so acres of the former Deramore Estate are utilised, secured on a 10,000-year lease and with an annual rent of £700. By kind permission of Lord

Location:
two-and-a-half miles south of Belfast

Type: parkland

Club administrator:
Kenneth H. Graham (01232-491693)

Club professional:
Maurice Kelly (01232-646714)

Best day for visitors:
ring in advance

1 R.M. Shearer's 'Shovel',
donated by the founder member
for Winter League's worst score!
2 Beautiful Belvoir, sweeping
uphill to the 3rd green.
3 The clubhouse commands
panoramic views of the course.
4 The tranquil Demesne setting.
5 Memento of another sport!

1

2

Deramore, the accommodating early landlord, the club is permitted to use his family coat of arms.

At Belvoir, the golfer is also aware that the war years have not left a scar. World War Two turned part of the course into a 'dig for victory' potato plot, and fairways were staked for fear that they might be utilised as landing strips in the event of an enemy invasion.

Invasions of a welcoming and friendlier nature that stand out in the club's colourful history were in 1949 and 1953, when Belvoir Park hosted the Irish Open Championship.

It is conservatively estimated that 10,000 people witnessed the emotional victory by Harry Bradshaw in 1949, as he avenged Bobby Locke's win earlier in the month in the infamous 'broken beer bottle' British Open Championship at Royal St Georges, Sandwich.

The Brad was moved to state that 'Belvoir Park is the finest inland course I've ever played on.'

The Scot Eric Brown had good reason to sing the praises of the club's 16th hole when he won the title in 1953. It is the last of five par threes and perhaps the most difficult in that it measures 204 yards. Yet Brown managed to score a hole-in-one and two birdie twos!

Set out in two convenient loops, the course has an abundance of character and special features. Meandering streams are seen to play a part at several holes.

For many, the lasting impression may well be provided by the 17th. If ever there was an exemplary par-four (449-yards) two-shotter strategically positioned in a round, the point is emphasised in this instance. It is what is

known as a delayed dog leg, with a forest and foliage along the left-hand side, thus placing additional premium on the driving position. The second shot is then a full carry over the stream and aimed at a pulpit green, which compounds the difficulty and lends credence to the theory that achieving par is a bonus … and the fact that lengthy periods can elapse without it yielding to a single birdie!

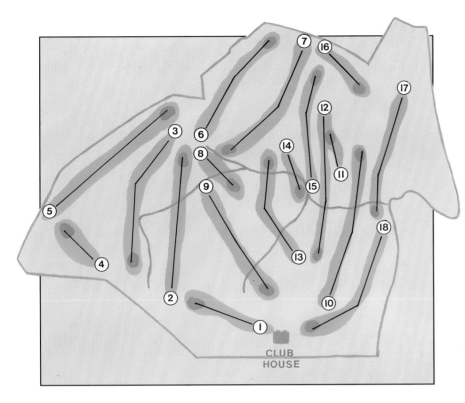

3

2

1 Good shot, sir! The ball nestles
close by the flagstick at the delightful
par-three 14th hole, with elevated
clubhouse at rear.

2 The sweep of the third fairway,
showing the dog-leg angle formed by
the line of trees.

3 A wide-angle view from Belvoir's
clubhouse balcony down the 10th
fairway, skirted by mature timbers.

Marker's Score	Hole No.	Yards	Metres	Par	Stroke Index
	1	284	260	4	18
	2	398	364	4	6
	3	428	391	4	2
	4	190	174	3	8
	5	517	470	5	14
	6	393	359	4	10
	7	440	402	4	3
	8	140	128	3	16
	9	484	443	5	12
OUT		3274	2991	36	
	10	480	439	5	5
	11	181	166	3	15
	12	462	422	4	1
	13	370	338	4	9
	14	167	153	3	13
	15	507	464	5	11
	16	204	187	3	7
	17	449	411	4	4
	18	407	372	4	17
IN		3227	2952	35	
OUT		3274	2991	36	
TOTAL		6501	5943	71	

CARLOW GOLF CLUB

~ YARDS: 6,428 ~ PAR: 70 ~

Given that the esteemed course architect Tom Simpson always contended that golf, as a game, is only seen at its best when there is at least as much necessity for brainwork as physical prowess, rest assured that Carlow reinforces his contention.

The layout refinement he introduced to the course in 1937 has proudly stood the test of changing emphasis in the game, for even if Carlow is of the shorter category by modern championship standards, the

Location:	two miles from town
Type:	parkland
Club administrator:	Margaret Meaney (0503-31695)
Club professional:	Andy Gilbert (0503-41745)
Best day for visitors:	avoid Tuesdays and weekends

consensus, quite simply, is that it is one of the finest inland courses in Europe.

Carlow, in fact, scores highly on two telling counts, for along with being a searching examination of golf it has an aesthetic charm of its own, and it is this amalgam that explains its popularity.

When you include the added virtue of renowned hospitality, then ready understanding is to hand of why the club has its enduring reputation as an ideal retreat 'away from it all'. Clubhouse restoration has suitably enhanced the offering.

Extensive, mature woods are a strong feature in a pleasant countryside setting where the unusually sandy soil has the noted bonus of allowing meaningful play all year round. This attribute has been at the heart of the successful stagings of such premier events as the Irish Professional Championship, won by Christy O'Connor Snr in 1975, and the Irish Amateur Championship, won by Mick Morris in 1977. Furthermore, each autumn the club hosts the reputable Midland Scratch

1 *The 9th green – climax of a classic hole.*
2 *Much-prized trophy for club competition: the Anderson Cup.*
3 *Hazards come in varying guises at Carlow, as illustrated here.*
4 *The subtle 16th green feature of the renowned Index 2 hole.*
5 *Carlow in times past.*

72-holes Trophy. It was started in 1950, when it was won by the great Joe Carr, and that the highest standard of winner has endured is underlined by the revealing statistic that, in the first 30 years of the event, only two players of non-international status managed to win.

It is significant also that when Britain's top amateur, Peter McEvoy, managed to plunder a 10-under-par winning effort of 68-69-67-66, the feat was greeted with incredulity. Such a low level of scoring around Carlow is quite remarkable.

The loop of holes from the 7th, heading back to and then away from the clubhouse, captures the heart of the course. The index-one seventh is considered hard enough not to require bunkering. The philosophy is understandable, given the demanding nature of the drive to a target area flanked on the left by penal rough and by a sentinel line-up of trees along the right-hand side. The second shot to the green (the hole measures 434 yards) also presents a tough examination of exact club selection as there is a deceptive, full carry to the elevated green.

A survey would surely show, however, hole 8 to be Carlow's *pièce de résistance*. An exhibit par four of 438 yards, the tee is perched precipitously on the highest point of the course. The drive is downhill, but to a fairway that gives the claustrophobic impression of being carved through the middle of a forest. For the second shot, the nerve must endure and combine with a clean strike off a downhill lie to a well-bunkered green – not easy!

That hazards come in varying guises at Carlow is then to hand as the threat of water rears its head. The 10th hole, by the clubhouse, at 304 yards is driveable. Yet theory conflicts with the practical, taking stock of a green guarded in part by a lake, right, and by a gathering hollow, left, which also contains water. Take note that OB lurks to the right of the green.

As the good Mr Simpson set out to forewarn: at Carlow, there is as much necessity for brainwork as for physical prowess.

1 *Nearly home – the green of the well-protected par-three 17th hole.*
2 *Beware of the notorious pond, en route to the 10th green.*
3 *Danger – you have been warned!*

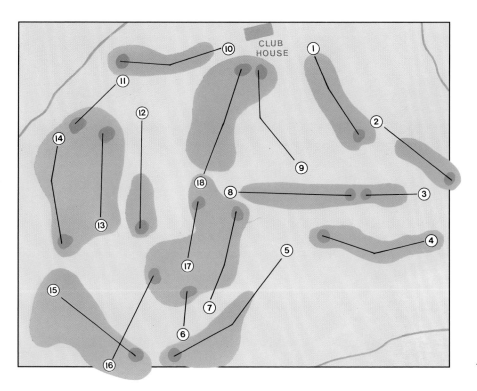

Hole	C/Ship Blue Tees Mtrs.	Medal White Tees Mtrs.	F'ward Yellow Tees Mtrs.	Par	Index	SCORE A	B
1	399	395	391	4	4		
2	285	275	269	4	14		
3	133	124	115	3	17		
4	338	333	328	4	9		
5	457	450	445	5	15		
6	167	163	159	3	12		
7	395	389	381	4	1		
8	399	390	369	4	6		
9	344	338	330	4	8		
Out	2917	2857	2787	35			
10	277	273	271	4	11		
11	389	381	371	4	3		
12	340	334	330	4	7		
13	154	150	145	3	16		
14	420	415	411	4	5		
15	343	334	325	4	10		
16	396	393	380	4	2		
17	139	134	127	3	18		
18	469	460	452	5	13		
	2927	2874	2812	35	IN		
	2917	2857	2787		OUT		
Total	5844	5731	5599		GROSS		
SSS	71	70	69		H'CAP		

4 *Sylvan setting for Carlow's* piece de résistance *8th hole.*
5 *Illustration of Mr Simpson's philosophy: brainwork, not power.*

CASTLEROCK GOLF CLUB
~ YARDS: 6,733 ~ PAR: 73 ~

With so much attention centred on the legendary links of Royal County Down and Royal Portrush, an unfair consequence is that some other well-deserving courses in Northern Ireland are often not afforded their share of recognition.

Castlerock falls into that category.

It is a decided injustice, as discerning golfers who have made the pilgrimage to the Causeway Coast will certainly testify to an unforgettable experience.

Castlerock itself is very beautifully situated in colourfully attractive, patchwork

Location:
six miles west of Coleraine

Type: links

Club administrator:
R.G. McBride (01265-848314)

Club professional:
Bob Kelly (01265-848314)

Best day for visitors:
avoid weekends

countryside. Its scenic qualities embrace the River Bann flowing out to the Atlantic, and also eye-catching views of Donegal and, on a clear day, towards Scotland and the Paps of Jura, together with the Isle of Islay. An ideal retreat in which to play golf.

History pervades the invigorating County Derry air, as the sand dunes through which part of the course wends its inviting way are said to be have been occupied by humans during the Neolithic and Early Bronze Ages. The links is rightly protected under the Historic Monuments Act of Northern Ireland.

The creation of an additional nine holes, shaped with uncanny vision from scrubland by the mouth of the river, has widened the appeal of the club. Long-serving club professional Bob Kelly is in no doubt about the merits of the added amenity. 'It is a natural,' he enthuses, and with interesting insight, he adds, 'There is no need to build bunkers … there are already enough hazards to overcome while hitting through the dunes.'

Castlerock Golf Club is long established as an important element in the hugely

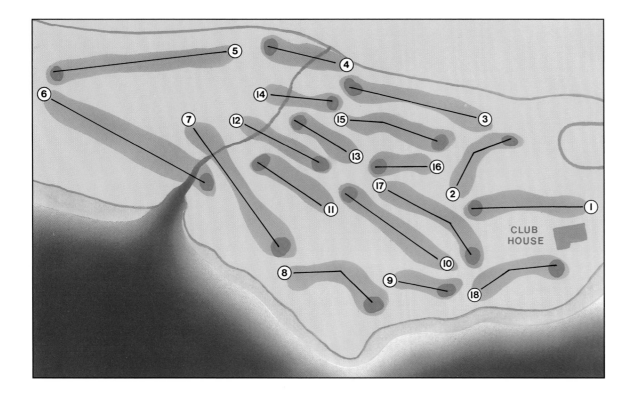

1 *Undulating Castlerock, looking back towards the welcoming tourist resort.*
2 *Added danger lurking at the infamous Leg of Mutton par-three 4th hole.*

successful Causeway Coast Tournament each year, when the neighbouring links of Royal Portrush, Portstewart and Ballycastle are also utilised in a four-round, four-course, roll-on stableford points competition.

The event, which has considerable international appeal, is sponsored by the 'Black Bush' label of Bushmills, the oldest whiskey distillers in the world, situated just up the road from the club.

Golf has been played at Castlerock since about 1900, and work has constantly been carried out to maintain a high standard of links, together with similarly caring devotion in ensuring that the spacious clubhouse is also of a standard sufficiently equipped to meet the needs of the club's ever-growing reputation.

While the sea and the river virtually surround the course, another characteristic is that a railway line bisects part of the layout, playing an integral part in the infamously celebrated – if not, indeed, controversial – 200-yards par-three 4th hole.

One of the single most talked about golf challenges in Northern Ireland, the hole is said to be called the Leg of Mutton by the romanticists and the Infernal Triangle by the more mathematically minded. The perception is that the tee is the apex, the green the base, and the sides are formed by the railway to the right and a stream to the left. You pick your club. You take your chance. And you stand and hope.

And to think you have yet to encounter the Burn, the Arm Chair and the Spion Kop.

The Causeway Coast derives its name from the spectacular Giant's Causeway, a strange mixture of boulders and stone pillars jutting out to sea. Legend tells that the phenomenon was the work of the giant Fionn mac Cumhaill, who built the causeway to use as stepping stones across the sea when he pursued the love of a fair maid of the Hebridean Island of Staffa.

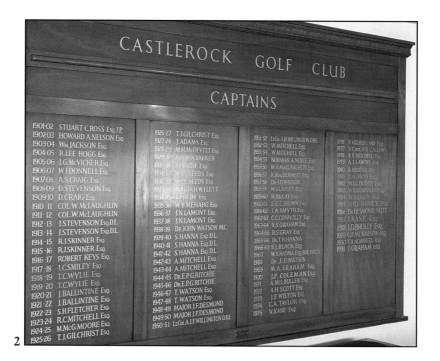
2

3

1

4

1 *Sacred territory among the dunes. A reminder that the area near the 16th green was occupied by man during the Neolithic and Early Bronze Ages.*
2 *A proud club's Roll of Honour.*
3 *Peaceful setting for the 7th green amid the dunes.*

5

6

7

MARKER	NUMBER	NAME	YARDS	YARDS	PAR	SCORE	INDEX
	1	KNOCKLAYDE	348	343	4		5
	2	SCONCE	375	366	4		9
	3	THE WHINS	509	493	5		13
	4	LEG O'MUTTON	200	184	3		11
	5	RAILWAY	477	472	5		15
	6	BURN	347	336	4		7
	7	ARMCHAIR	409	407	4		2
	8	BULLDOZER	411	400	4		3
	9	QUARRY	200	193	3		17
		OUT	3276	3194	36		
	10	FAIRY DELL	391	386	4		4
	11	COASTGUARDS	509	485	5		16
	12	SPION KOP	430	420	4		1
	13	SWALLOW HILL	379	363	4		14
	14	CORNER	192	182	3		8
	15	HOMEWARDS	518	510	5		6
	16	SUMMIT	157	145	3		18
	17	INISHOWEN	493	485	5		12
	18	MUSSENDEN	342	330	4		10
		IN	3411	3305	37		
		OUT	3276	3194	36		
		TOTAL	6687	6499	73		

4 Be forewarned ... and be up!
5 Castlerock's perpetual challenge.
6 Valley setting for the 12th green.
7 New clubhouse in a splendid
setting hard by the town of
Castlerock.

CONNEMARA GOLF CLUB
~ YARDS: 7,272 ~ PAR: 72 ~

As you exit from the 18th green at Connemara Golf Club, there is a notice which reads, 'Thank you for playing Connemara Golf Club. Hope you enjoyed your game. Life Membership available. Full details: contact secretary-manager.' Such is the fast-growing appeal of Ireland's most westerly championship course (it is a case of next stop New York!) that there is a queue at secretary-manager John McLaughlin's office door in search of subscription forms.

No course in such a short period of time has captured the imagination as has lovely Connemara, established only since 1973. It is situated within scenic sight of the Twelve Bens mountain peaks on an isthmus at Ballyconneely Bay, just near the narrow, stone-walled road from the alpine town of Clifden, generally regarded as the 'Capital of Connemara'.

When the course was first opened, the doubting Thomases felt that its remote location would militate against its chances of ever becoming established in a nationally recognised context.

Driven by a determined bunch of committed golfing afficionados, most conspicuously by local curate Fr Peter Waldron, the club's pioneers always had faith in the project design by Eddie Hackett. At around 7,272 yards off the championship stakes, it was originally perceived as an uninteresting hard slog. Yet the designer managed to break the monotony of the many flat areas by sagacious employment of advantageous high ground, into which

Location: nine miles from Clifden

Type: links

Club administrator:
John McLaughlin (095-23502)

Club professional:
Hugh O'Neill (095-23502)

Best day for visitors:
avoid Sunday mornings

C'Ship Metres	Medal Metres	Winter Metres	Par	Stroke Index	Hole	Score A	Score B
349	331	328	4	6	1.		
385	366	354	4	8	2.		
154	145	143	3	18	3.		
358	335	325	4	12	4.		
360	342	339	4	14	5.		
193	175	164	3	10	6.		
531	482	451	5	16	7.		
438	418	381	4	2	8.		
408	344	293	4	4	9.		
3176	2938	2778	35		OUT		
398	383	379	4	7	10.		
171	151	142	3	17	11.		
416	399	351	4	1	12.		
196	180	161	3	5	13.		
483	460	417	5	15	14.		
367	349	346	4	9	15.		
417	370	367	4	3	16.		
491	468	445	5	11	17.		
496	475	447	5	13	18.		
3435	3235	3055	37		IN		
6611	6173	5833	72		TOTAL		
75	73	71			S.S.S.		

quick endorsement, and the World Left-Handers' Championship has since been held here.

By common consent, the Connemara course has many outstanding virtues. But if you prefer a less demanding game, then new holes laid by the seashore are not as daunting a challenge.

The sting is in the tail at Connemara, as a six-holes finishing flourish incorporates three par fives!

The stretch kicks off with an awesome par three, the 13th, measuring 198 yards off the medal tee, and it is best not to contemplate the notion of tackling the vast chasm between tee and green from the back mark of 215 yards!

The more manageable 14th, a par five of 523 yards, follows to a raised green. The par three 15th of 383 yards then requires a mid iron to be hit into a spectacularly set plateau green. The 16th is a longer par four, where water on the left must be circumnavigated, and there is no let up as the final two holes

were skilfully positioned many inspired greens locations.

The staging of the Irish Professional Match Play Championship in 1980, won by the Ryder Cup player Des Smyth, brought

1 *Breathtaking start to the back nine against the background of the Twelve Bens.*
2 *... And to finish, a renowned par five.*

are back-to-back par fives of over 530 yards apiece.

Then, when you finally catch your breath, you will come away from Connemara knowing you were in a fight, but no doubt enticed by the inviting offer on the notice board to the side of the final green!

🍀 *Not far from the course is Kylemore, the enchanting abbey belonging to the Benedictine nuns, and closer still are the ruins at Derrygimlagh Bog of the first trans-Atlantic wireless station, established by the Marconi company, where aviation pioneers Alcock and Brown made their bumpy landing at the climax of*

1 Perpetual memento of key founding member, Fr Peter Waldron.
2 An irresistible offer!

1

their historic non-stop trans-Atlantic flight on 14–15 June, 1919 from St John's, Newfoundland.

🍀 *If summer at Connemara by the shimmering Atlantic Ocean and golden sandy beaches is bliss, the locals will swear that May-June is another sight to behold as the links becomes a picture of yellow, blue and purple wild flowers.*

THANK YOU FOR PLAYING
CONNEMARA
HOPE YOU ENJOYED YOUR GAME
LIFE MEMBERSHIP AVAILABLE
FOR DETAILS PLEASE CONTACT
SECRETARY MANAGER

2

3

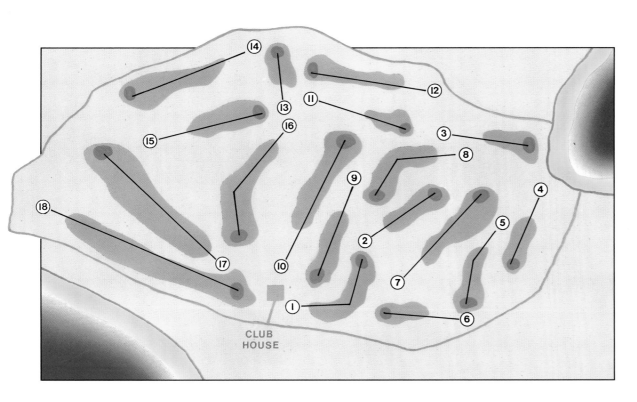

5

4

6

7

3 The subtle dog-legging 1st hole, heading away from the Atlantic.
4 Neighbouring alternative attractions.
5 An ideal clubhouse location offering panoramic views and respite by the 18th green.

6 Scenic reprieve of mountain backdrop, as seen from the green at the Index 2 8th hole.
7 Atlantic reminder from Ireland's most westerly lighthouse, Slyne Head, presented by lighthouse keeper and club President Eugene O'Sullivan.

CORK GOLF CLUB

~ *YARDS: 6,725 ~ PAR: 72* ~

It is by uncanny coincidence that, just as Dublin's premier club, Portmarnock, was discovered by a couple of questioning fishermen, Cork Golf Club should similarly come into being.

The most esteemed club in Cork city and its envirous came into existence as a consequence of a chance sailing trip by existing members of the club (then sited at Cóbh Junction), who were out boating and who intuitively formed the opinion that the land mass jutting into Lough Mahon, in the estuary of the River Lee, was, indeed, an ideal site for golf.

Those pioneering co-members of Royal Cork Yacht Club, the oldest such club in the

Location: five miles east of the city

Type: parkland

Club administrator:
Matt Sands (021-353451)

Club professional:
Peter Hickey (021-353421)

Best day for visitors:
telephone for appointment

world, made their discovery in about 1898, and although under their yachting charter no admiral was allowed to bring 'more than

two dishes of meat for the entertainment of the club … nor more than two dozen wine to his treat … except when my Lords, the judges, are invited,' to visiting golfers the door is always open.

Another telling contribution made in the emergence of the newly sited Cork club at Little Island was by the hand of that illustrious course architect Dr Alister McKenzie. He had been commissioned in 1927 to work at Lahinch, and the decision to utilise his great flair at Cork was wisdom amply rewarded. Mind you, the additional land into which the course was extended had already received the blessing of the great Harry Vardon when he came to play an exhibition in 1909.

Granted by nature the marvellous prospect of clear views across Cork Harbour or towards the Tower Castle at Glanmire (the line of sight for your drive at the eighth hole), the Cork club is also outstanding for the fact that much of the parkland spread requires the golfer to circumnavigate a huge limestone quarry.

On the attractive river stretch, from behind the 3rd green, along the classically sited 4th and 5th holes and on by the ragged

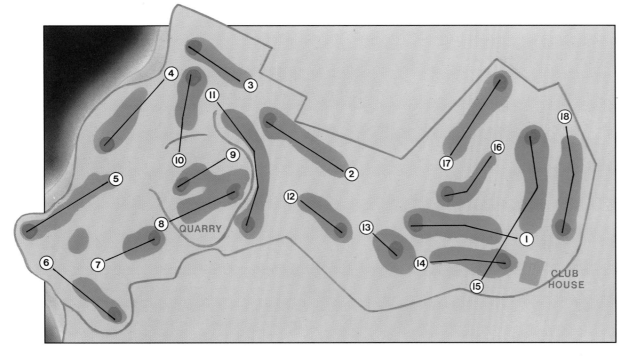

1 *The Irish County Shield proudly displayed.*
2 *The 12th green and fairway.*
3 *Dr Alister Mackenzie, who was retained in 1927 to advise on course improvements.*

shoreline to the 6th tee, the mind's eye can easily accommodate the scene around the turn of the century, when quarried limestone was transported on barges to the mouth of the estuary to be transferred to ships heading across the Atlantic.

Local lore says that many of the skyscrapers in New York and Boston can trace a limestone origin to that quarry in the middle of Cork Golf Club.

The par-three 7th hole and the drive to the 8th are played from the floor of the quarry, and its intimidating effect remains chillingly in focus throughout the 8th and onwards in the playing of the long, curving par-five 11th hole.

Even then, with your back to the chasm, there is little reprieve, because McKenzie's signature is most pronounced in the nature of Cork's much-acclaimed finishing climax.

That takes the form of a 'no prisoners' crescendo of five straight par fours, sweeping back down towards the imposing stone-faced clubhouse and away again, to return via a magnificent 17th hole played from a high tee across a long carry to a narrow fairway, and on then to the 18th, where the out-of-bounds boundary wall confirms the enduring suspense.

Fittingly for such a superb package, Cork Golf Club has played host to many great events. The Irish Open Championship was played here in 1932, when English professional Alf Padgham just held out in the face of a course record 66 from countryman A.H. Davis. When the Irish Native Professional Championship was staged in 1940, the then unknown Fred Daly,

seven years later to become Ireland's first and, to date, only British Open champion, emerged to stamp his potential. Since then, Neil Coles won the Carrolls International Tournament of 1965 and Tom Horton won the RTV Rentals tournament in 1968.

Of course, no mention of Cork Golf Club can be made without reference to Jimmy Bruen, of the 'loop' swing pattern. The club's most illustrious son, who died just prior to his 52nd birthday in 1972, was, in the opinion of most, the greatest Irish golfer ever. It was said that between 1936 and 1946 he might, indeed, have been the best golfer in the world.

One of Bruen's many feats was his ability to drive Cork's first hole!

1

2

1 The 5th green nestles close by the ragged water's edge of the Lee estuary, from where limestone was transported for loading onto ships heading across the Atlantic.
2 Dramatic cliff setting for the superb short par-four 6th hole.

| Hole | METRES | | | Par | Index |
No	Blue	White	Green		
1	340	335	330	4	7
2	460	442	435	5	13
3	244	244	239	4	17
4	411	402	384	4	1
5	510	504	460	5	9
6	300	272	260	4	15
7	169	158	151	3	5
8	379	374	368	4	3
9	178	170	152	3	11
Out	2941	2839	2755	36	
10	374	358	350	4	2
11	454	450	443	5	14
12	289	286	275	4	12
13	157	149	138	3	18
14	397	380	372	4	8
15	383	366	360	4	4
16	323	315	276	4	16
17	360	335	320	4	10
18	387	370	362	4	6
IN	3124	3009	2896	36	
Total	6065	5848	5651	72	
S.S.S	72	70	69		

3 *Treasured memorabilia saluting the late legendary Jimmy Bruen, Cork's most famous player.*
4 *Colourfully attractive castle and estuary form a backdrop at feature holes.*
5 *The club's trophies.*

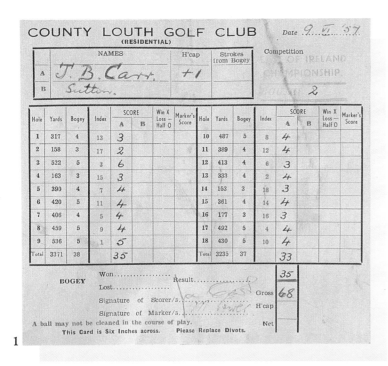

1

2

3

CO. LOUTH GOLF CLUB

~ *YARDS: 6,763 ~ PAR: 73* ~

Thankfully a pair of golfing aficionados were drawn to the uncharted territory at the fishing village of Baltray back in 1892, when they set sail pondering the merits of a golf course. Otherwise, we might never had had the County Louth Golf Club. Divine Providence, the members would have you believe!

Mr G.H. Pentland, together with John Gilroy, a retired banker of Scottish origin, had been baulked by the disfavour of local inhabitants in laying a few holes nearby and were awestruck by what they discovered. An incredulous Mr Gilroy (who was to become Ireland's first scratch handicap player), exclaimed, 'Here was I trying to make a course out of poor material when, less than a mile away, there was one of the best pieces of golfing ground in the world!'

It is now easy to understand his enthusiasm, as history has shown that the County Louth club's course at Baltray (by which village name it is also popularly known) is, indeed, long established and accepted as one of the very best links in Britain or Ireland.

Central to the cause was the foresight of the committee in the mid-1920s in inviting

1 *Proud achievement by J.B. Carr, who is synonymous with the club's East of Ireland championship.*
2 *The founding members of a famous club.*
3 *The view from behind the green at Baltray's lovely par-three 15th hole.*

Location:
five miles north-east of Drogheda

Type: links

Club administrator:
Michael Delaney (041-22329)

Club professional:
Paddy McGuirk (041-22444)

Best day for visitors:
avoid Tuesdays and weekends

Hole	Blue Course	White Course	Green Course	Score A	Score B	Strokes Rec'd	Par
1	433	423	410			3	4
2	476	476	476			17	5
3	544	534	519			9	5
4	344	334	324			15	4
5	158	148	143			13	3
6	531	521	505			7	5
7	163	153	148			5	3
8	407	397	387			11	4
9	419	409	399			1	4
Out	3475	3395	3311				37
10	398	388	375			4	4
11	481	476	476			16	5
12	410	410	387			2	4
13	421	408	376			6	4
14	332	322	308			12	4
15	152	142	137			18	3
16	388	375	360			8	4
17	179	169	169			10	3
18	521	492	476			14	5
In	3282	3182	3064				36
Out	3475	3395	3311				37
Total	6757	6577	6375				73

Tom Simpson to update and indeed reconstruct the original design, which had been laid out by a Scottish professional with the odd name of Snowball.

At that time Simpson was noted for the artistry of his work in the development of major British courses at Sunningdale, Royal Porthcawl and Muirfield and, in company with the well-known lady player of the day, Molly Gourlay, he also performed his skills at Carlow and Ballybunnion where, too, he admirably adhered to his philosophy of never having two greens alike.

A flamboyant man of considerable private means, Simpson spurned a career in law so that he could indulge his passion for golf course architecture. This he did in the grand manner, travelling everywhere in a chauffeur-driven Rolls-Royce. His work at County Louth could truly be said to be the top of the range.

It is odd, therefore, that the wonderful links, which is the home since 1941 of Ireland's premier 72-holes amateur stroke play event, the East of Ireland, has not been feted in accordance with its quality.

The noted British golf architect and writer Donald Steel said, 'From the moment you turn off the main road in Drogheda and head for Baltray, there is an ever increasing feeling of remoteness and beauty so essential to a great seaside links.'

It has also been said, in generous respect, that County Louth is a Portmarnock that has not quite grown up!

In terms of comparison, the club stands favourably any test. If anything, it scores

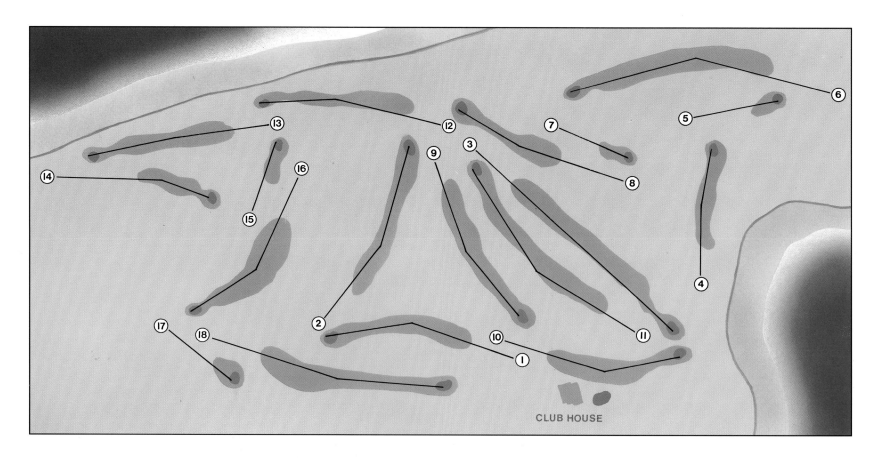

1

superior marks by way of its detached setting. Thatched cottages survive to indicate what an 18th- and 19th-century Irish fishing village looked like, with the classic links nestling peacefully amid the high dunes by the mouth of the River Boyne, leading to the ancient trading town of Drogheda. Furthermore, it has the advantage of offering accommodation

2

in the handsomely refurbished clubhouse.

Baltray's power on-course is widespread. Contrasting features are embodied in the devilish 3rd hole, a true gem among five par fives. It is inherent, too, in a sequence of cunning par fours (try the 1st, the 9th and the 12th for starters) and it is highlighted also in the pleasure there is to enjoy in the four marvellously varied one-shotters, as underlined by the 5th hole.

The special atmosphere of the place also seems enhanced by family tradition and the obvious involvement of the village inhabitants, for nowhere does the family strain run deeper or greater than in this golfing hotbed. There are the Reddens, the Garveys, the Gannons, the McGuirks, the Smyths and other representatives of the household names the district has weaned in producing many of the finest amateur and professional men and women golfers Ireland has known.

1 *The 410-yards, Index 2 par four …*
the tee awaits!
2 *Wild daisies lend their appeal to*
this seaside links course.

6

7

3 Undulating greens and dunescape
features at County Louth.
4 It's a long way home at the par-five
11th hole!
5 The added colour of pink broom.
6 Helpful markers to great holes.
7 The putting green and the
clubhouse.

5

An illustration of the close-knit nature of
the community is that the Ryder Cup player
Des Smyth is married to Vicki Reddan,
daughter of the famous Curtis Cup and Irish
International Clarrie, whose husband, Val, is
the hospitable club steward and whose son
Barry, himself an Irish international, is one
of the leading lights of the club.

*It was the ladies who first brought fame to
the club – when Clarrie Tiernan won the Irish
women's title in 1938 – a championship subsequently won on a record 15 occasions by the
legendary Philomena Garvey.*

*Family tradition has been proudly main-
tained at County Louth, where club professional Paddy McGuirk, a winner of the major
Carrolls International Tournament in 1973, has
succeeded his late father, Michael, in the role.*

CO. SLIGO GOLF CLUB

~ YARDS: 6,603 ~ PAR: 71 ~

'The Land of Heart's Desire' was how the immortal Yeats brothers, W.B., the writer, and J.B., the painter, described their beloved County Sligo. In the golfing sense, what they portrayed on canvas and with the pen is beautifully captured at the County Sligo Golf Club, or Rosses Point, as it is more commonly known.

Is there another golfing location in Ireland, indeed anywhere in the world, enjoying a more restful setting, or commanding a greater panorama of beauty? We doubt it, encompassing as it does Yeats' 'Bare Ben Bulben's Head' and Drumcliffe Church, where the great poet lies buried, his simple limestone memorial slab bearing an epitaph of his own composition:

> 'Cast a cold Eye
> On Life, on Death.
> Horseman, pass by!'

Cast an eye across to Sligo town, sheltered beneath the Ox Mountains, or take account of the vast sweep of the Atlantic Ocean westward, and to the south the sandy beaches of Strandhill (where there is another fine 18-hole course), or of Knocknarea, upon the summit of which lies the resting place of Queen Méabh of Connacht, and which is itself a haven for archaeologists.

The noted television commentator Peter Alliss said, 'I did think Rosses Point was something people should go and look at and I think they will come away marvelling at this beauty.'

Location:	five miles west of Sligo town
Type:	links
Hon. Secretary:	Ronnie Dunne (071-77186)
Club professional:	Leslie Robinson (071-77171)
Best day for visitors:	avoid Tuesdays and weekends

Star player Bernhard Langer summed up its appeal by declaring, 'I went to play one round – and stayed two weeks.' The late and esteemed Cecil Ewing, the Point's most famous golfing son, was moved to suggest that 'when the winds blow, the only hiding place is to be found back in the clubhouse.'

These are perceptive words of wisdom from a man whose exploits locally, and as an Irish team player and Walker Cup ace, helped to create a greater awareness of the classic Sligo golf links. His 10 victories, in face of a personal battle for supremacy with his great foe, Joe Carr, from the mid-1940s to 1950s formed much of the rich folklore of the West of Ireland Amateur Open Championship, staged at Eastertide at Rosses Point since 1923. All of Ireland's leading amateur players compete each year.

A recent clubhouse refurbishment programme, whilst reverently maintaining the quaint Tudor exterior that lends its own touch of identification, has greatly upgraded the Sligo club.

On the course there is conscientious care to maintain the best traditions of a supreme links, discovered by inquisitive members of the old Sligo Militia in 1894 and extended

1 *In the immortal words of Cecil Ewing, the club's most famous player: 'When the winds blow ... the only hiding place is in the clubhouse.'*
2 *Hill-top view towards the famous links to the 6th and 14th greens.*

and improved upon around 1920 by Colt and Alison, the foremost golf architect of the time. Its unique setting combines a staircase-type contrast of clifftop plateaus which has the effect of presenting a multitude of varying shots.

Of the old-fashioned, out-and-back layout variety, Rosses Point has many memorable holes. The downhill par-five 2nd; the eternally proud par-four 8th; the clifftop 12th and the downhill par-three 13th (making

Hole	Marker's Score	Name	C'ship Metres	Medal Metres	Par	Stroke Index
1		Greenlands	347	339	4	8
2		Barr na Séide	278	273	4	11
3		Metal Man	457	448	5	15
4		Gan Gaineamh	150	150	3	12
5		The Jump	438	428	5	17
6		Bomore	387	339	4	6
7		Ewing's Profile	385	377	4	1
8		The Churn	374	374	4	5
9		Cast A Cold Eye	153	138	3	13
		OUT	**2969**	**2866**	**36**	
10		Ben Bulben	351	346	4	10
11		Lissadell	366	366	4	3
12		Light House	448	441	5	14
13		Wrynne Point	162	156	3	18
14		Mahon's Burn	394	359	4	4
15		Through the Gap	367	360	4	7
16		Knocknarea	196	172	3	16
17		The Gallery	414	385	4	2
18		Christy's Farm	336	325	4	9
STABLEFORD POINTS OR PAR RESULT		**IN**	**3034**	**2910**	**35**	
		OUT	**2969**	**2866**	**36**	
		TOTAL	**6003**	**5776**	**71**	

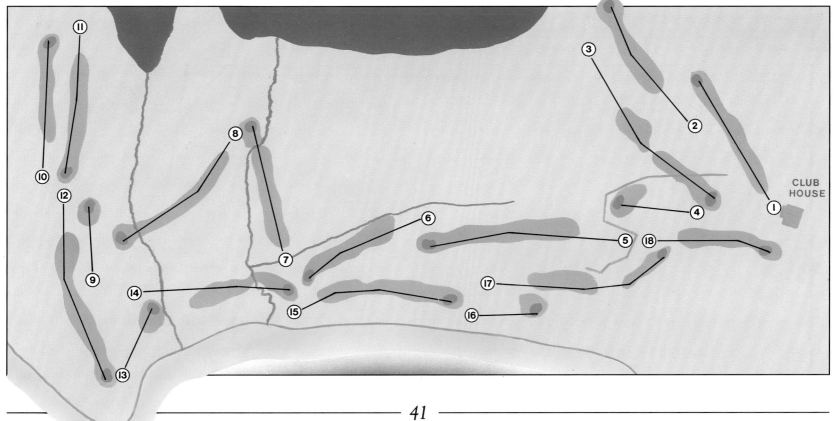

1

2

1-2 *The legend of Rosses Point tells of the Metal Man, line of sight at Hole 3 to Dead Man's Point, and a landmark signalling safe passage.*

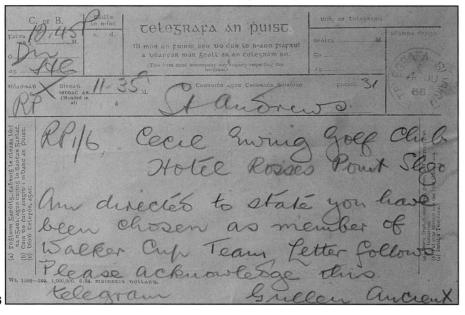

3

4

5

6

3 *The telegram notifying Cecil Ewing of his Walker Cup team selection.*
4 *Period clubhouse entrance.*
5 *Stonewall, the par-three 9th gem.*
6 *The welcoming refurbished clubhouse.*
7 *Tenth green in the shadow of Ben Bulben.*

7

sure to stay out of the stream partly encircling the green), have carved their own special niches.

It is from the 13th hole inwards, hugging the seashore, that Rosses Point unveils a finishing stretch – as highlighted by the 17th – that, win or, more likely lose, will lure you back to try again.

One of the great landmarks at Rosses Point is the Metal Man, on Perch Rock, with outstretched hand sternly signalling a safe passage through the channel. 'The Rosses Point

man who never told a lie,' Yeats noted of the distinctive 12-foot-high figure in place since 1822 at Dead Man's Point, following the occasion when a seaman died as a ship was leaving port. He was buried at sea with indecent haste, lest the tide be missed! Unsure whether the poor unfortunate was really dead, his hurrying shipmates buried with him a loaf of bread, in case he should revive!

The purest and most perfect manifestation of the classic Rosses Point links might be in the playing of the 17th hole. Here is a golfing challenge

the likes of which you will not find anywhere else. Aptly named the Gallery, the wickedly difficult 455 yards par four firstly demands that the drive on low-lying flat ground be so measured as to stay clear of some rough terrain which forms the foothills of a steep, right-to-left dog-leg climb to a tilted green perched austerely at the base of yet another craggy tier of cliff. The accomplishment of a par has a therapeutic effect, for which you will be grateful as you climb again to steer the 18th hole blind drive over the ravine from which you have emerged!

DONEGAL GOLF CLUB

~ *YARDS: 6,868 ~ PAR: 73* ~

By the wind-tossed edge of the great Atlantic Ocean, Donegal Golf Club stands defiantly in face of the destructive ravages of the sea. Every winter, concerned members hold their breath in fearful anticipation as the relentless pounding of cruel seas further threatens to eat into the magnificent links. At one vulnerable point adjacent to the low-lying 8th green and 9th tee, an area 60 yards deep by 200 yards long has been washed away since the club moved to the headland setting in 1973.

That the wearisome battle has not broken the hearts of the club members is evident in their determination to raise the £25,000 which is required each year to continue the fight against erosion.

In order to reach the club you will have negotiated a narrow passage through a national forest to a tranquil setting which lends itself to the aptly titled holes such as Pinewood, Fairy Bath, Hare's Croft, Badger's Sett and the Larks.

Full appreciation of this hidden treasure in such appealingly close vicinity to the Bluestack Mountains can be savoured from the hospitable shelter of the spacious clubhouse, where sensible and plentiful utilisation of glass affords a spectacular view

Location:
nine miles from Donegal town
Type: links
Club administrator:
John McBride (073-35054)
No professional
Best day for visitors: avoid Sundays

of the longest golf course in the Republic of Ireland.

Course architect Eddie Hackett, Ireland's best known, made his design all the more inviting by the clever format of the front inner running along the outer boundary in an anti-clockwise direction, with the back nine clockwise on the inner track.

The Valley of Tears is the gauntlet you must endure to fully appreciate the challenge. This is the name given to the par-three 5th hole of 185 yards, playing from a plateau tee to a plateau green, and with trouble all along the way in the form of rough, as well as frightening bunkers.

The experience is the starting point to a particular feature stretch of the course, which embraces a demanding tee shot from above the sandy beach to the par-five 6th hole. In turn, this is followed by the requirement of another good positional drive to the crest of the hill at the 7th, and then on to the

1 *Blue Stack mountain backdrop to*
the par-three 5th green.
2 *In the Valley of Tears.*
3 *The treasured clubhouse scrapbook.*
4 *History maker – Máire O'Donnell.*

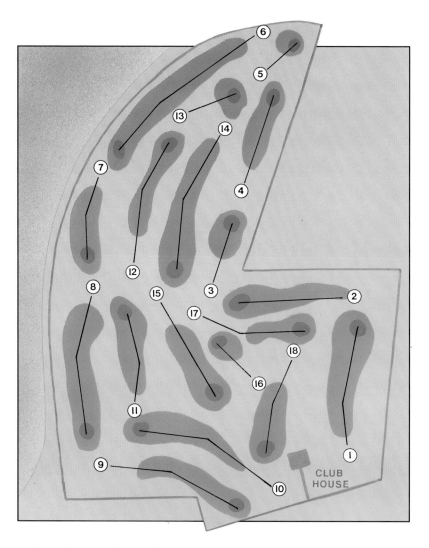

exhausting par-five 8th, measuring 544 yards off the high-rise championship tee and aimed firmly towards Moyne Hill, beyond which lies a valley at a point where you become all too aware of Donegal's possible fate at the hands of the cruel sea.

🍀 *A piece of golfing history was made by the Donegal Golf Club when Máire O'Donnell was elected captain of the B and I team for the Curtis Cup match against America in Denver, Colorado, in 1982. She became the first native of the Republic of Ireland to be so honoured.*

🍀 *Donegal is Ireland's largest Irish-speaking county and is also famous for its woven tweeds, the very colours and patterns of which reflect the district's wildly beautiful scenery. The Temple family, proprietors of the local top-label manufacturing company Magee, have been at the core of the golf club's history, with the premier annual open fixture hosted by the Donegal club being the Magee Scratch Trophy.*

THE ORIGINAL LANDS OF THE DONEGAL GOLF COURSE AT TULLYCULLION, WERE PRESENTED BY THE TEMPLE FAMILY IN MEMORY OF ROBERT TEMPLE. MAGHERABEG HOUSE. DONEGAL. DIED 20TH MAY. 1958.

1 *Granite resistance against the problems of coastal erosion.*
2 *Clubhouse plaque in memory of a dear friend and honoured family at the heart of the club.*
3 *Beautifully manicured course and the approach to the 9th green.*

Hole	LENGTH IN METRES		
	WHITE Course	ORANGE Course	GREEN Course
1	478	468	458
2	379	369	341
3	173	163	163
4	380	370	363
5	170	160	152
6	473	463	438
7	352	344	334
8	499	492	492
9	306	296	286
Out	3210	3125	3027
10	320	310	310
11	340	330	334
12	503	493	493
13	145	128	120
14	479	454	448
15	370	362	362
16	209	199	189
17	323	313	313
18	344	334	334
In	3033	2923	2903
	3210	3125	3027
	6243	6048	5930

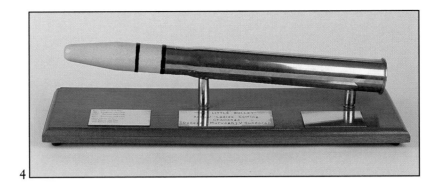

4 *The 'Little' Bullet, presented by army personnel for competition between the ladies of Donegal and Bundoran. There is also a 'Big' Bullet for competition between the men.*

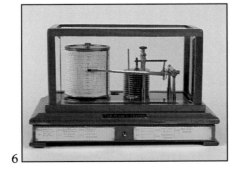

5 *Donegal's majestic putting surfaces.*
6 *The Magee Trophy, presented for the annual Scratch Cup competition.*
7 *The strategically placed clubhouse.*

DRUIDS GLEN
~ YARDS: 7,026 ~ PAR: 71 ~

It is a measure of the recognition of Druids Glen as one of the best new golf course creations that within a year of its official opening it was deemed good enough to host the Murphy's Irish Open Championship.

At first glance, the Ryder Cup star Eamonn Darcy, later to join as club professional, was sufficiently moved to exclaim: 'Augusta may have its Amen Corner, but at Druids Glen they have created a complete litany of golf hole thrills – it's just unbelievable'.

Cascading waterfalls; white, shimmering sand in irregularly shaped bunkers; the remorseless vision and challenge of water; multitiered greens; extravagant earth-moving and landscaping, are components not synonymous with the traditional face of Irish golfing architecture.

Location: 20 miles south-east of Dublin city

Type: parkland

Club administrator: Denis Kane (01-2873600)

Club professional: Eamonn Darcy

Best day for visitors: visitors welcome

1&2 Views of the 18th hole (1) from behind the green, and (2) heading towards the green to the imposing backdrop of the historical clubhouse. 3 Place of ancient worship – the unique site for the par-three 12th hole.
4 Flavour of the signature 13th hole.

At Druids Glen, these virtues capture the innate spirit of a quite extraordinary course, where designers Pat Ruddy and Tom Craddock have gone a long way towards meeting the brief to create Ireland's best inland course!

Endorsement has been rapid since the captivating Druids Glen was unveiled in 1995, most conspicuously by the many world stars who have played at the mystically named course, so suitably nestled in County Wicklow's much-famed Garden of Ireland.

Heralded as something akin to a golfing Garden of Eden, the par-71 championship course of 7,026 yards is further complemented by its unique clubhouse. Woodstock House, a stately manor, was built around 1760 and in its magnificently restored state it features classic columns

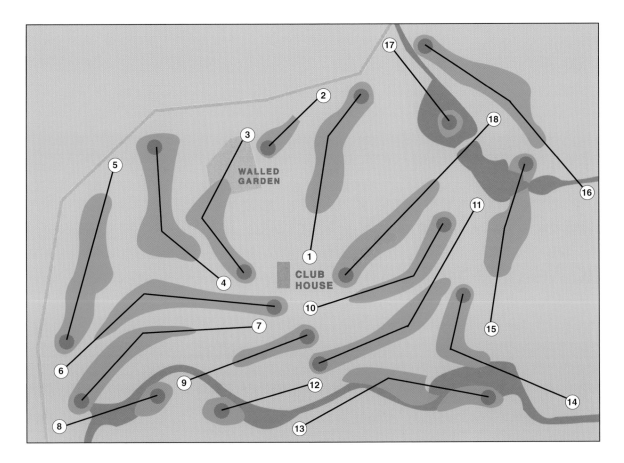

No.	Yards			Par	Index
	Blue	White	Green		
1	445	427	389	4	4
2	190	174	162	3	8
3	339	330	328	4	16
4	446	417	398	4	7
5	517	492	484	5	17
6	476	456	413	4	2
7	405	392	377	4	6
8	166	152	140	3	11
9	389	369	350	4	15
Out	3373	3209	3041	35	
10	440	401	372	4	10
11	522	512	512	5	13
12	174	155	148	3	12
13	471	461	451	4	1
14	399	333	294	4	14
15	456	395	369	4	9
16	538	481	475	5	18
17	203	178	133	3	5
18	450	422	419	4	3
In	3653	3338	3173	36	
Tot	7026	6547	6214	71	

3

4

and exquisitely ornate plasterwork on ceilings and cornices.

Amid an on-course floral background that forms a blaze of hues and colours in all seasons, the acclaimed rolling parkland course is a gem. At the core of its appeal is the rich variety of par threes.

The tone is set at the second hole, varying between 160 to 190 yards, where the shot is broadly based on the approach to the infamous Road Hole at St Andrews.

Furthermore, you can savour the notion of playing at Augusta, taking account of the 8th of 166 yards across water and then the equally stunning 12th played in the opposite direction.

The finishing crescendo further complements the package. The 17th, a stand-alone par three of 205 yards, features an island green and the 18th, played against the backdrop of the imposing clubhouse, is a never-to-be-forgotten climax, played uphill

to a tilting green staunchly protected by not one, or two, but three lakes that cascade over granite-stoned weirs, one atop the other. It is an awesome climax.

Druids Glen, or Gleann na Draoite in Gaelic, owes its name to the pagan high priests who worshipped in the thickly forested countryside in the fifth century before Christ. A druid's altar stands on a hillside overlooking the 12th green.

THE EUROPEAN CLUB

~ *YARDS: 6,885 ~ PAR: 71* ~

Considering the fact that, of the approximately 42,000 golf courses in the world, there are only about 152 courses of genuine links texture, the value of the discovery of the European Club needs no qualification. Quite simply, it is a treasure.

It was the first major golf links to appear on Ireland's East Coast in over 100 years and by any yardstick it is of sufficient merit to bear comparison with the best.

The ambitious dream come true of golfing aficionado Pat Ruddy, it has been readily endorsed by some of the greatest

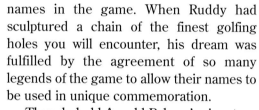

Location:	25 miles south of Dublin at Brittas Bay
Type:	links
Club administrator:	Pat Ruddy (0404-47415)
Club professional:	none
Best day for visitors:	visitors welcome daily

names in the game. When Ruddy had sculptured a chain of the finest golfing holes you will encounter, his dream was fulfilled by the agreement of so many legends of the game to allow their names to be used in unique commemoration.

Thus, behold Arnold Palmer's signature on the 8th hole, Gary Player's on the 11th, Tom Watson's on the thrilling 17th, Lee Trevino's love of the tantalising par-three 6th, Gene Sarazen relishing the 14th, another par three, and Sam Snead providing an insight into his golfing philosophy by putting his name to the 4th hole.

Innovation is very much at the core of Pat Ruddy's brainchild. The European Club, for example, has twenty holes and a man-made water feature!

Two loops of ten holes feature the additions of par threes between the 7th and 8th, and the 12th and 13th. Why? Simply because the configuration of the dunes presented the potential, and the golfer duly reaps the bonus! Therefore, you are playing against a par of 77 over 7,490 yards, converting to 7,165 yards and par 71 for 18 holes.

The greater debate centres on the creation of Lake Lawrenson fronting the 18th green. It is a sting in the tail that some argue is out of character. Yet, queries the designer, what of St Andrews and the Swilcan Burn; Royal St George's and the Suez Canal; Carnoustie and the Barry Burn?

It is a measure of the quickly established reputation of the 'young' European Club,

2

Hole	Ch'ship	Medal	Par	S.I.
1	390	370	4	10
2	160	155	3	18
3	480	470	5	16
4	430	410	4	2
5	395	385	4	8
6	185	180	3	14
7	435	400	4	1
8	410	395	4	5
9	420	400	4	12
10	415	395	4	7
11	385	375	4	11
12	420	400	4	4
13	540	530	5	15
14	165	160	3	17
15	380	370	4	9
16	415	375	4	13
17	390	380	4	3
18	445	425	4	6
Total	6,885	6,580	71	

• *all distances in yards*

which was officially unveiled on St Stephen's (Boxing) Day, 1992, that it is already favourably compared with Ireland's acknowledged great links courses. Indeed the European Club is a worthy addition to the hallowed pilgrim spots, such as Ballybunion, Portmarnock, Royal County Down, Royal Portrush, Lahinch and Waterville, that invariably appear prominently in the 'best' lists of most discerning judges.

All the best virtues of the links course are amply encompassed in the club. Rugged dune, deep natural sand hazards, sea breezes and large, undulating, fast-running greens are the true characteristics of this oasis by the Wicklow coastline.

An added merit is the scenic dividend afforded by the clever design concept. A glimpse of the sea is ever to hand. Two feature holes, the par-four 12th (perhaps the most classic hole on the links) and the following par-five 13th of 539 yards, each run hard by the beach, which is an integral part of the course. The routing of the holes through the dunes further maximises the powerful setting.

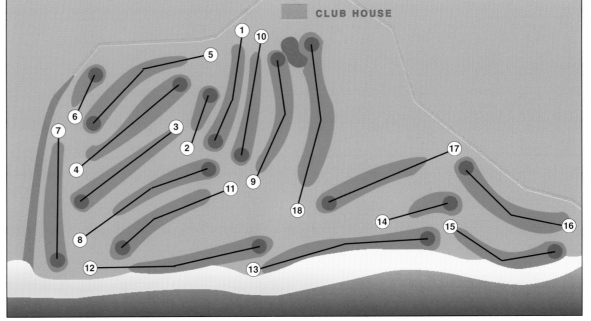

The European Club is a private club with a visitor-friendly policy. Guests are welcome daily, "providing they have basic playing skills and a knowledge and appreciation of the etiquette of the sport".

1 *The par-four 10th hole illustrates the classic links virtue of this golfing treasure.*
2 *The fabulous 11th hole, endorsed by Gary Player and played against the backdrop of Arklow Bay.*

FOTA ISLAND

~ YARDS: 6,910 ~ PAR: 71 ~

While Fota Island was unveiled as one of Ireland's spanking new golfing creations in September 1993, a fascinating backdrop is that golf may well have been played in this unique setting 100 years before!

Historians point to a report in the *Belfast Newsletter* stating that 'a correspondent of one of the London dailies wrote that he had noticed the opening game on a course at Fota Island, Cork, in February 1883 and had observed that the ways of Scoticism had crossed the Channel and travelled as far as Cork where the game had been initiated with great success'.

Remains of the old course are no longer readily apparent, yet the historical contention may be given substance by the fact that the area immediately in front of Fota House is known as 'The Links Fields'.

What cannot be disputed is the current stature of Fota, nestled tranquilly in Cork Harbour, a few minutes drive from Cork City, which itself is steeped in a golfing tradition. It amply meets the toughest yardstick and bears comparison with all the other fine parkland courses that in recent years have come along to enhance Ireland's golfing image.

A sister property to the renowned Mount Juliet resort in County Kilkenny, the determination also to bring major events to Fota is underlined by a significant upgrading programme to a course co-designed by Christy O'Connor Jnr and the British amateur golfing ace Peter McEvoy.

Location: nine miles east of Cork City

Type: parkland

Club administrator:
Kevin Mulcahy (021-883700)

Club professional:
Kevin Morris (021-883710)

Best day for visitors:
visitors welcome daily

The excellently appointed course, with a telling par 71, is the centrepiece of a 780-acre wooded estate, listed among the Inventory of Outstanding Landscapes of Ireland. Its unique ambience is further highlighted by the fact that the neighbouring landscape is home to the Fota Wildlife Park and Arboretum.

Conspicuous by its welcoming large greens, its grassy swales, pot bunkers and strategically located water features, Fota also stands out for its virtue in combining a new look with a traditional old feel,

1

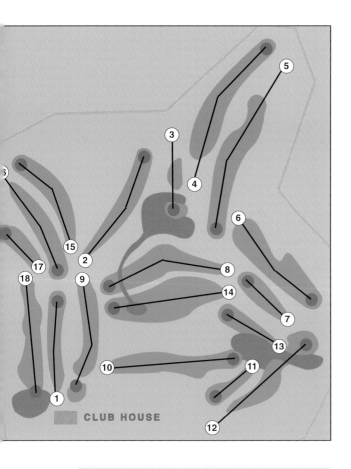

Hole	Blue	White	Green	Par
1	394	363	348	4
2	454	427	404	4
3	191	182	136	3
4	547	520	503	5
5	536	509	475	5
6	372	353	326	4
7	181	172	144	3
8	485	477	476	4
9	426	397	386	4
10	503	503	476	5
11	170	161	151	3
12	427	389	373	4
13	202	191	183	3
14	412	392	371	4
15	465	434	408	4
16	417	399	386	4
17	219	202	191	3
18	509	482	470	5
Total	6,910	6,553	6,207	71

• all distances in yards

something that further raises the senses as to its forgotten history.

Fota's endearing qualities also take account of comparisons with St Andrews and Augusta. If the use of a double green is borrowed from the Old Course at St Andrews, the thrill of Augusta can be savoured in negotiating a par three of 180 yards, with water guarding the left-hand approach to a tilting green that mischievously falls to the lake. There is the further thrill of experiencing the treachery of the signature 10th hole, like its counterpart at Augusta. The hole winds down a tree-lined slope with water, rather than sand, guarding the green. A most fulfilling encounter!

2

3

1 A tranquil setting for the unique, stone-walled clubhouse.
2 The finishing hole to a course that is ideal for staging major events.

4

3 The mischievous par-three 3rd hole, infamously known as Little Island.
4 A reflection of the captivating Fota Island course beside the 18th green.

GRANGE GOLF CLUB
~ *YARDS: 6,034 ~ PAR: 68 ~*

The notion of a golf course opening with successive par threes, including as many as six one-shotters, and with a par of 68, conjures images of a prospective easy ride. Definitely not so at Grange!

This beautifully styled course, with a wood-panelled clubhouse of Bavarian appearance, and set on the slopes of Kilmashogue, a foothill of the Dublin Mountains, belies its appearance on paper, pretty much in accordance with the time-honoured principle that the proof is in the eating.

Certainly on the short side by modern championship standards, the course is nonetheless cleverly structured, as it is in a confined space amid plentiful trees and shrubbery. Bunkering is a key factor, there is a river in play for the short pitch to the 2nd hole, and the same river also has to be negotiated in the approach to the much-documented 18th.

In every sense Grange shows the clever architectural hand of James Braid. He was acknowledged as the leading course architect of the 1920s and 1930s, and of the hundreds of courses he either remodelled or designed from scratch, the opinion is fairly unanimous that his work here stands favourable comparison with any of them.

At Grange, the monument to the canny old Scot (a five-times British Open champion, be it noted) was his perception in endorsing the oddity of a golf course starting with two par threes. That was the notion of the original architect, Tom Hood, in 1910, and

Location:
five miles south-west of Dublin
Type: parkland
Club administrator:
Séamus O'Donoghue (01-4932889)
Club professional:
Barry Hamill (01-4932889)
Best day for visitors: midweek

when Braid's reputation was such that he was invited to re-draw the plans in 1927, his eagle eye wisely demanded absolutely no change to the 1st, the 2nd and the 18th.

A par three of roughly 222 yards is fairly self-explanatory. But when it demands your opening shot uphill, and with a line of un-broken trees hard to the right, as well as green-side bunkering, the realisation of the overall theme of the challenge quickly dawns.

The 2nd hole is a less daunting effort, requiring much less club over much less distance, yet you will probably be playing above yourself if you somehow manage a 3-3

1 The club's glittering trophy showcase.
2 Berry-bearing mountain ash en route to the rising 3rd fairway.
3 An animal scratching post survives on the 5th fairway as a reminder of times past, when animals were allowed to graze.

1

2

3

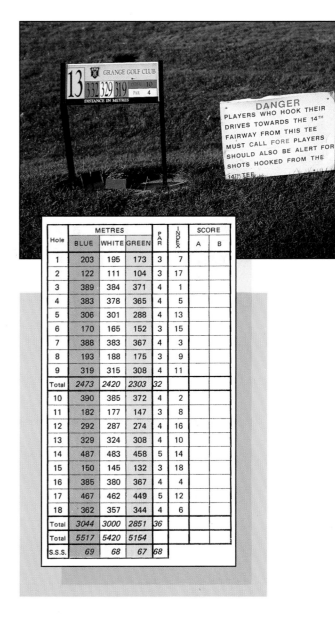

Hole	METRES			PAR	INDEX	SCORE	
	BLUE	WHITE	GREEN			A	B
1	203	195	173	3	7		
2	122	111	104	3	17		
3	389	384	371	4	1		
4	383	378	365	4	5		
5	306	301	288	4	13		
6	170	165	152	3	15		
7	388	383	367	4	3		
8	193	188	175	3	9		
9	319	315	308	4	11		
Total	2473	2420	2303	32			
10	390	385	372	4	2		
11	182	177	147	3	8		
12	292	287	274	4	16		
13	329	324	308	4	10		
14	487	483	458	5	14		
15	150	145	132	3	18		
16	385	380	367	4	4		
17	467	462	449	5	12		
18	362	357	344	4	6		
Total	3044	3000	2851	36			
Total	5517	5420	5154				
S.S.S.	69	68	67	68			

start. Indeed, the short holes at Grange have the tendency to throw up more fives than twos.

The 11th is another case in point. It is of brilliant configuration, playing from a low-lying tee box across a lengthy chasm (the hole measures a touch under 200 yards), and rising to another well-bunkered green.

Of course, it is not only the par threes that engage the senses. On the contrary, two par fours particularly stand out.

To the inclining ground at the lovely 10th, take aim with the drive much towards the steeple of the quaint stone-walled church beyond the course boundary on the right. Don't be drawn too far right, as a towering chestnut impedes the line to the green.

In contrast, the 18th hole falls downhill and requires that the drive be long and straight. Even if you have managed to thread the ball through the trees, you now face the examination of a clean strike, mostly off a downhill lie, for a shot that must carry over the widest stretch of the Kilmashogue River.

This is one of the great finishing holes, where the meek will 'lay up' – and the mighty indulge!

Contingency plans are to hand should the club lose any of its holes in the cause of motorway construction. Additional ground purchased by the club in 1976 means that

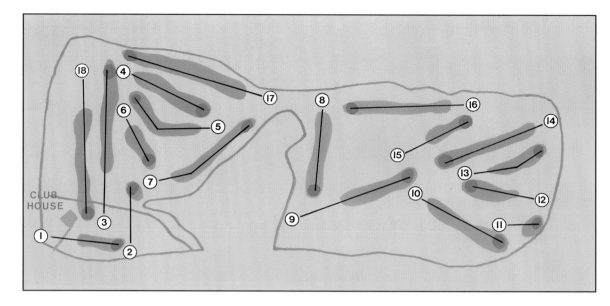

new holes have been maturing and are ready to be incorporated into the main course.

Dr David Sheahan, the Grange club's most famous member, was a three-times Irish amateur champion who also had the rare distinction of beating an international field of professionals to win the Jeyes Pro-Am Tournament at Royal Dublin in 1962.

During World War I the club was taken over as a training ground by the military, who had the use of the course until 12.30 p.m. each day.

4 Prized club championship cup, presented in 1939 by Dr R.E. Davitt.

3

4

5

6

1 The delightful wood-panelled clubhouse of Bavarian appearance, a unique design in Ireland.

2 The granite-walled Kilmashogue River guards the well-trapped 18th green.

3 A clubhouse tribute to Dr David Sheahan, Grange Captain in 1993, holding aloft the Irish Amateur Close Trophy, won in 1960, 1966 and 1970.

5 Caricatures of club celebrities attending the first Captain's dinner.

6 A view of the 11th green in the foothills of Kilmashogue.

HERMITAGE GOLF CLUB

~YARDS: 6,637 ~ PAR: 71 ~

What strikes you most about the lovely Hermitage Golf Club is its total seclusion amid a circle of majestic trees, yet it is only five miles along the new western motorway from Dublin city. And, if you should require it, a bus passes the front gate.

The accessibility of the rolling, leafy retreat of prize oaks, wych-elms and limes partly explains its popularity. The fact that it takes the inviting form of an excellently manicured, classic parkland design, commanding additional scenic patchwork views and the sight of the venerable River Liffey, completes a package that makes Hermitage one of the most inviting places to play.

The Liffey holds a key role as it meanders close by the back of the feature par three 10th hole. It is also 'in play' throughout the equally infamous 11th, a par five of fully 565 yards which also rates highly on every discerning golfer's pecking order of great holes.

Welcoming hospitality at a notably good social club is another endearing quality, although at Hermitage the 19th hole is, actually, just that! An idiosyncrasy peculiar to the place is that there are nineteen holes.

Location: five miles west of Dublin city

Type: parkland

Club administrator:
Tom Spelman (01-6268491)

Club professional:
Simon Byrne (01-6268072)

Best day for visitors:
any weekday except Tuesday

There are two 10th holes: each one a par three and each one a gem.

The showpiece 10th, and one of the most pictured holes in the game, is a dramatic case of the firmly struck tee shot – lofted with a wedge or thereabouts by some, or optionally punched on a lower trajectory by others – from the side of the clubhouse, descending fully 60 feet in a sheer drop to a green pitched at about 140 yards length. It's a thrilling hole to play if you don't suffer from vertigo, and you will fondly cherish your par, just as you will in winter time, when the adjacent 'other'

1 Tee view at the much-documented par-three classic 10th hole in a serene wooded valley, with the River Liffey in the background. It is one of two 10th holes at Hermitage!
2 Outline of the hazard-strewn route to the green at the testing par-five 11th hole.

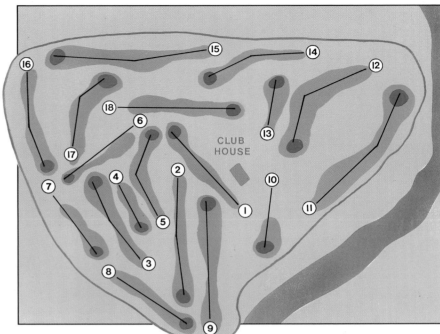

10th hole is introduced, which is of pretty similar design if not quite as precipitous.

Local Hermitage folklore is well embroidered by stories of success – though mostly of failure! – at the 10th hole. Pride of place belongs to Norman Drew. Playing in the 1959 Irish Dunlop Tournament, the one-time Walker and Ryder Cup player was six shots adrift of Harry Bradshaw going into the last round. What had all the appearances of being a formality for 'the Brad' was, however, dramatically turned on its head as Drew missed the green at each of the first three short holes on the course, the 4th, 7th and 10th, only to chip into the cup each time for twos. This remarkable feat back-boned a course record 66 and gave virtuoso Drew a two-shots win.

Further recognition that the setting of Hermitage provides one of the best inland courses came when the European Ladies' and European Youth's Team Championships, in 1979 and 1984 respectively, were staged there, and if a growing lobby of opinion had its way, the Golfing Union of Ireland might move to bridge a gap to 1914, when it was the venue for the National Amateur Championship.

At a time in the game when the role of the course architect is a high-tech, high-profile and highly expensive exercise, it is worth noting that the Hermitage course, pretty much as you see it today, is the work of a man

chronicled only as Mr McKenna, from Portmarnock. The man with no initial was engaged to do the design once this pristine land was acquired around 1905 for the sum of £3.10.0 (£3.50) an Irish acre. There was a clubhouse thrown in for good measure!

In those far-off days it was called the County Dublin Golf Club, but this was soon changed to Hermitage. The club actually takes its name from the Hermits' Caves, which

can still just about be seen in the wooded area between the 9th fairway and the 10th green.

Local tradition insists to this day that the white-robed figure of the Lady Agnes moves through the trees at ghostly dawn reciting the Ballad of the Hermit of Lucan:

Within a cave in time of old,
A Hermit did abide,
Where Lucan rears its holy fane,
And River Liffey rolls her tide.

3

	71	70	69	SSS		Score	
Hole	Blue	White	Green	Index	Par	A	B
		Metres					
1	279	273	265	18	4		
2	407	400	399	4	4		
3	346	330	325	6	4		
4	161	155	147	16	3		
5	326	305	300	12	4		
6	290	285	281	14	4		
7	206	199	190	8	3		
8	402	380	375	2	4		
9	460	457	452	10	5		
OUT	2877	2784	2734		35		
10	155	146	142	15	3		
11	512	492	447	9	5		
12	380	374	370	1	4		
13	180	172	167	11	3		
14	327	320	317	7	4		
15	455	430	416	17	5		
16	368	362	354	3	4		
17	380	366	302	13	4		
18	400	370	365	5	4		
IN	3157	3032	2880		36		
Total	6034	5816	5614		71		

4

PAR 3. S.I. 15
155 m.
146 m.
142 m.
135 m.

This is but one of many legendary or historical associations concerning the beautiful Hermitage course. Within the cell itself, the story goes, is the Lovers' Chair, or Wishing Stone, believed to be jealously protected by a time-honoured spell. Beware!

1 *Rear view of the 10th hole, rising steeply back to the clubhouse.*
2 *Bunkering is a feature, as shown on this fairway.*
3 *The 'Bunkered Pike Story' at the 19th hole (see text right).*
4 *The lovely clubhouse, nestled among the pines.*

Extracts from early club minutes: 'It was agreed to pay caddies one shilling per barrow load of sheep droppings collected on the links.'

'Champagne not to be included on menu for Captain's Dinner.'

The case of the Bunkered Pike with a bed spring protruding from its jaws, and how it came to be encased in a glass at Hermitage, richly embellishes anecdotes at the club's 19th. The story dates back to a stormy day in 1939, when the Liffey overflowed its banks and the fish was stranded in a bunker with the wire embedded in its jaws.

THE ISLAND GOLF CLUB
~ *YARDS: 6,658 ~ PAR: 71* ~

The time is long past when the only means of access to the Island Golf Club was, as the title indicates, by boat, but old-timers fondly remember the short but hazardous trip across the choppy estuary from the village of Malahide in pursuit of a game on a quaint and old-fashioned links.

Tradition may well have changed, what with a new roadway and entrance on the other side of the peninsula and, indeed, a virtually new course, but what endures is the club's great sense of values.

It readily explains why the Island is one of the favourite haunts of visitors wanting to play the game in the best atmosphere and on the best links land conditions.

Where once it was correct to say that the course essentially comprised small greens (however good to putt on) that were largely hidden from view, a conscientious campaign, designed to coincide with the Centenary Year of 1990, has resulted in the introduction of seven brand-new holes, which have been cleverly blended into the best of the original layout.

Location: four miles north-east of Dublin airport

Club administrator:
John Finn (01-8436462)

Club professional:
Kevin Kelliher (01-8436462)

Best day for visitors:
avoid weekends and afternoons, except Fridays

1 Tide out – time to play golf!
2 Tide up – the only means of getting to The Island in days past.
3 The exhilarating view from the par-three 13th's tee across Broadmeadow Estuary to Malahide village.
4 Demure Miss Jameson, champion Island player of the 1920s.

4

Traditionalists will be relieved to note, however, that such long-standing favourites as the Broadmeadow, the Andes, Old Clubhouse, the Prairie and the Bowl, just to pick a handful, have survived.

Indeed, the fearsome 13th, an outrageous par three of 212 yards, looking across Broadmeadow Estuary to the mainland, is a treasured hole that leaves a lasting impression; all the more so as it is likely that you get to play it when the wind is whipping up the cliff face from the sea.

This is the point of the course where the renowned O'Brien family used to ply their rowing-boat trade, and a further glimpse into the past is observed at the old landing berth to the rear of the original first tee. It is now the 14th. But, you may well ask, where is the fairway? This has got to be the narrowest par four in the game!

Golfers with an appreciation of times past, and you can't help being touched by nostalgia at the Island, also savour the story of the Cricket Field, now the 11th hole. It seems the cricket immortal W.G. Grace brought over a group of friends to play golf. The visitors were beaten in a match against the members, and when it was then suggested that the sides should play a cricket challenge, a makeshift pitch was duly rolled and marked. It is recorded that the famous W.G. was bowled first ball!

The Island is a warmly welcoming club, where part of its rich folklore is that it was conceived by a syndicate of bachelors, yet it was courtesy of the women members, when

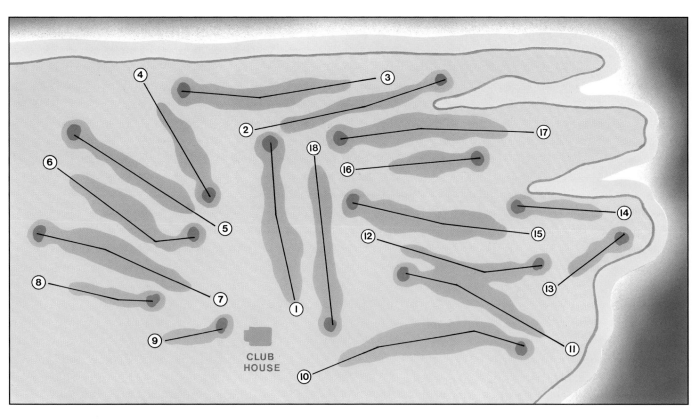

S.S.S		72	70	P A R	I N D E X
		METRES			
		MEDAL	CLUB		
1	PARTRIDGE HOLLOW	396	359	4	5
2	POLE HILL	363	341	4	7
3	LAMBAY	405	389	4	1
4	POT	320	309	4	11
5	DESERT	336	315	4	9
6	RIDGE	300	279	4	13
7	TOWER	403	399	4	3
8	WELL	282	272	4	15
9	BOWL	159	151	3	17
	OUT	2964	2814	35	
10	QUARRY	500	481	5	14
11	CRICKET FIELD	284	282	4	18
12	VALHALLA	379	366	4	4
13	BROADMEADOW	191	196	3	8
14	OLD CLUBHOUSE	315	301	4	16
15	PRAIRIE	507	467	5	12
16	ANDES	140	137	3	10
17	IRELAND'S EYE	366	344	4	6
18	BOULIA FIELD	407	381	4	2
	IN	3089	2955	36	
	OUT	2964	2814		
	TOTAL	6053	5769		

1

2

3

they were eventually admitted, that the club gained its reputation.

The first major competition held was the Irish Women's Championship of 1911. It was won by a member, Mabel Harrison. She went on to win six times, and a further insight into the affairs of the club was that up to 1929 Miss Harrison and two other associates, Patsy Jameson, of whiskey family fame, and Mrs Allison Hall between them won the Irish championship title 12 times! In defer-ence to such heady achievement, it was entirely fitting that the high point of the club's Centenary Year celebrations was the staging of the Irish Women's Championship.

Because of the 'syndicate' influence, the club remained the exclusive preserve of those 'invited to join', and it was only about 50 years ago that the barriers were relaxed and the running of the club handed over to the general members.

How things have changed for the better, although there is a respectful appreciation of times past preserved. A virtue that under-lines why the Island stands alone.

1 *History-maker Mabel Harrison's exploits led to Centenary Year highlight.*
2 *Island boatman bids adieu.*
3 *Far from the madding crowd – the tranquillity of the 15th fairway.*

4 *Blazing cotton lavender by the 1st tee.*
5 *Outline of the old landing jetty, once the only means of access to the links.*
6 *The narrowest fairway in Ireland, seen from the back of the 14th green.*
7 *Wild orchids abound on the links.*

KILDARE HOTEL
AND COUNTRY CLUB
~ YARDS: 7,101 ~ PAR: 72 ~

The fact that the Kildare Hotel and Country Club has been awarded an exclusive five-star rating in the round of hotel designations from the Automobile Association underlines the very essence of the 'K' club at Straffan.

It is the centrepiece of the luxury £30 million development, the first hotel in Ireland to win a five-star rating in the history of the A.A. awards, and it is ample reward for the appetite-whetting properties of the 18-hole championship golf course.

Since the project embraces the combination of Ireland's best-known businessman, Dr Michael Smurfit, and the legendary golfer and course architect Arnold Palmer, further qualification is hardly necessary.

What has evolved, quite simply, is a deluxe standard of such lavish quality that nothing quite like it has been previously witnessed in Ireland. In terms of golf-oriented opulence, the 'K' club has emerged to give Ireland a brand-new image.

One of the great attractions of the high-class facility is that it does not merely comprise golf. Other provisions of the resort, set in 330 acres of prime landscape in the heart of the famed horse county of Kildare (the National Stud and the internationally renowned Curragh racecourse are just down the road), include tennis, horse riding, swimming, archery, croquet, and trout and salmon fishing.

The property, with the superbly reno-

Location:	four miles from Naas
Type:	parkland
Club administrator:	Paul Crowe (01-6273111)
Club professional:	Ernie Jones (01-6273111)
Best day for visitors:	ring for appointment

vated and historical Straffan House as a commanding hotel highlight, is bordered by one ambling mile of the River Liffey. If this lends itself invitingly to the attraction of fishing, the clever golf course design means that the river is teasingly brought into play at critical points in the round.

Arnold Palmer's design concept, in fact, sees water in play on ten specific occasions, such is the strategic manner in which he built the spectacular course to bring the river directly into play at holes 7, 8 and 17, together with the adroit employment of several man-made lakes.

'What I have done is to offer the option of an extremely testing course off the back tees, or the playing of a more modest length from the middle to forward tees,' says the acclaimed course designer. 'Either way, I feel I have guaranteed that the player will get enjoyment from his efforts, and that is the design concept that myself and Michael Smurfit set out to provide,' Palmer continues.

1 *The Club President's Trophy.*
2 *Elegant Straffan House,*
centrepiece of the luxury complex,
which traces its origins to the year
A.D. *550, when Strongbow granted it*
to the Fitzgeralds, ancestors of the
Dukes of Leinster.
3 *The 17th green by the banks of the*
River Liffey.

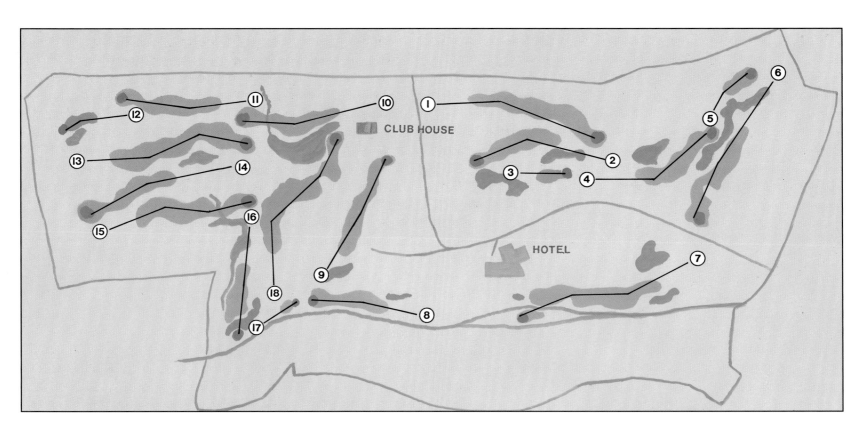

1

2

The true measure of the course is captured in these sentiments. Fulfilled by his efforts, and reflecting proudly on his work while standing on the terrace of the elevated clubhouse, sited immediately behind the 18th green, Palmer mused, 'We could draw for 100 years and still not come up with as good a vision.'

Given that the yardstick of a good golf course has always been the test of how many clubs will be used in a round, the growing consensus is that Palmer's course, formally opened with due pomp and ceremony in July 1991, is a great one.

'The shots required to be played vary in satisfying diversity from a wholesome emphasis on lengthy, straight tee shots to deft and discerning approach play, requiring much finesse,' says Ernie Jones, the club professional.

Hole No. 7, Inish More, the longest on the course at a whopping 608 yards, embraces many wonderful and spectacular features. A double dog-leg, the daunting challenge endures after two well-placed long shots, calling for an assured pitch over the River Liffey.

1 *No. 13, designer's pick, outlining the troublesome right-hand flank.*
2 *The gracious clubhouse reception, with a portrait of the visionary Dr Michael Smurfit and the course designer, Arnold Palmer.*

3 *The spectacular Straffan House Hotel.*
4 *The lily pond at numbers 3 and 4.*
5 *Clubhouse restaurant and veranda.*
6 *'Twas down by Anna Liffey' (Peadar Kearney) … to the 7th green.*
7 *Everything explained!*

4

5

METRES						
HOLE	BLUE	WHITE	GREEN	YELLOW	PAR	INDEX
1	529	512	490	450	5	5
2	373	351	334	312	4	9
3	160	148	127	117	3	17
4	368	351	317	306	4	7
5	196	177	168	156	3	15
6	406	376	352	335	4	11
7	553	543	513	483	5	3
8	341	306	306	306	4	13
9	395	392	369	353	4	1
Out	3321	3156	2976	2817	36	
10	380	364	345	325	4	6
11	374	361	339	339	4	12
12	157	132	132	132	3	18
13	521	497	497	468	5	4
14	380	358	343	327	4	14
15	410	376	358	340	4	2
16	361	339	339	319	4	10
17	141	120	120	120	3	16
18	474	460	437	425	5	8
In	3198	3007	2910	2795	36	

6

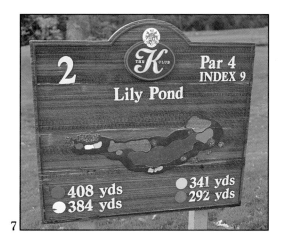

7

The river stays in play for the full length of the arching 8th hole; and then, on the back nine, be forewarned of the potentially destructive part that water can play from hole 15 to the spectacular climax of the 18th, the appropriately labelled the Hooker's Graveyard!

KILLARNEY GOLF AND FISHING CLUB
~ KILLEEN ~ YARDS: 7,027 ~ PAR: 73 ~
~ O'MAHONY'S POINT ~ YARDS: 6,767 ~ PAR: 72 ~

It was once said that writing about Killarney is akin to writing about St Andrews. There surely is nothing new to say.

The equally perceptive analogy has been made that, whereas St Andrews is golf, golf is but a segment of Killarney, for St Andrews is the home of golf and Killarney is the home of beauty!

Heaven's Own Reflex is what the locals would have you believe and, with characteristic sparkle in the eye, Kerry folk will further convince you that one of the world's most visited tourists resorts is 'the end product of what the good Lord Almighty can do when He's in a good mood!'

Location:
two miles from town centre

Type: lakeside

Club administrator:
Tom Prendergast (064-31034)

Club professional:
Tony Coveney (064-31615)

It is, of course, self-evident that this quite enchanting setting by the shimmering lakes, as immortalised in song by Bing Crosby, and in the bewitching valley of the mount-ainous and multi-coloured Macgillycuddy's Reeks, is, indeed, a tapestry most beautifully embroidered by nature's hand.

The distinguished international stars Nick Faldo and Payne Stewart were prominent among the club's new converts in 1991, when Killarney hosted the Carrolls Irish Open Championship for the first time.

The honour of Killarney being seconded to the rota for big-time tournament promotion highlighted one of the club's very virtues: the dilemma of which of their two fine courses to utilise. That the vote came down in favour of the newer, lakeside Killeen course, essentially designed by club stalwart and local personality, the good Dr Billy O'Sullivan, in no way diminishes the everlasting expression of Sir Guy Campbell when he built the original course, now known as O'Mahony's Point.

Plans are in hand for the creation of a third course on a site in the woods back towards the town, on higher ground commanding ever greater views. Could it be possible?

1 Heaven's Own Reflex, the locals will tell you, and who would argue with such a view from the tee of the lovely par-three 10th lakeside hole?
2 By Killarney's lakes and fens … the view from the back of the 1st green on the Killeen course, looking back across Lough Leane to the clubhouse and Macgillycuddy's Reeks.

A disappointment in not employing O'Mahony's Point for the Irish Open Championship was the sadness that the fabled par-three 18th hole could not be used, for it is a do-or-die climax to a round of golf that can have few equals. An inlet of the lake extends from the tee to the apron of a green, more conspicuous for its length than its accommodating width, which is sheltered by 150-foot-high pines and surrounded by flowering blazes of rhododendron. 'A nice place to die,' as someone once said.

By coincidence, it is another short hole, the infamous 6th, that also provides a lasting impression of Killeen. Of much the same length, at around 196 yards from the back, the full carry of An t'Oileán is a more exact science. The steeply raised green is an island, completely surrounded by water, so that the tee shot, and it will take a long iron (at least!), must be hit with conviction – and be made to stay on the dome-shaped putting

2

1

1 The grand finale to O'Mahony's Point – par three, 179 metres, all carry and fraught with danger. The ultimate challenge – an everlasting memory of 'a most memorable finishing hole in golf', according to the legendary Gene Sarazen; 'great golf and visual splendour combined,' commented Tony Jacklin.

surface. Though it is a short hole, there are more fives registered than twos!

Not easy, as with so many of the other feature holes on the more difficult Killeen course. But then beautiful Killarney adequately compensates. Make an early booking.

In June 1957, a golfer playing at Killarney sliced his ball into the lake. It struck and killed a trout that happened to be rising at the time. His friend waded in to retrieve the ball – and the trout.

	O'Mahony's					Killeen			
	METRES			Index		METRES			Index
No.	Blue	White	Par		No.	Blue	White	Par	
1	341	316	4	13	1	334	301	4	12
2	404	386	4	1	2	347	320	4	8
3	431	395	4	5	3	179	160	3	18
4	141	137	3	15	4	378	316	4	4
5	448	439	5	9	5	436	436	5	10
6	360	347	4	3	6	178	148	3	14
7	169	157	3	11	7	441	367	5/4	2
8	532	495	5	7	8	378	358	4	6
9	296	288	4	17	9	349	332	4	16
Out	3122	2960	36		Out	3020	2738	36/35	
10	344	336	4	8	10	155	150	3	15
11	426	411	4	2	11	465	452	5	11
12	215	167	3	16	12	434	384	4	5
13	435	435	5	10	13	404	392	4	1
14	344	344	4	4	14	353	326	4	17
15	251	246	4	18	15	375	362	4	9
16	463	435	5	12	16	454	448	5	13
17	373	340	4	6	17	339	331	4	3
18	179	162	3	14	18	390	371	4	7
In	3030	2876	36		In	3369	3216	37	
Tot.	6152	5836	72		Tot.	6389	5954	73/72	
s.s.	72	70			s.s.	73	71		

2 Pure Champagne is the name given to the 10th green in memory of a ceremony in 1969, when Dr Billy O'Sullivan invited visiting media to drink champagne in celebration of its construction. The bottle and a scroll lie buried beneath the green!

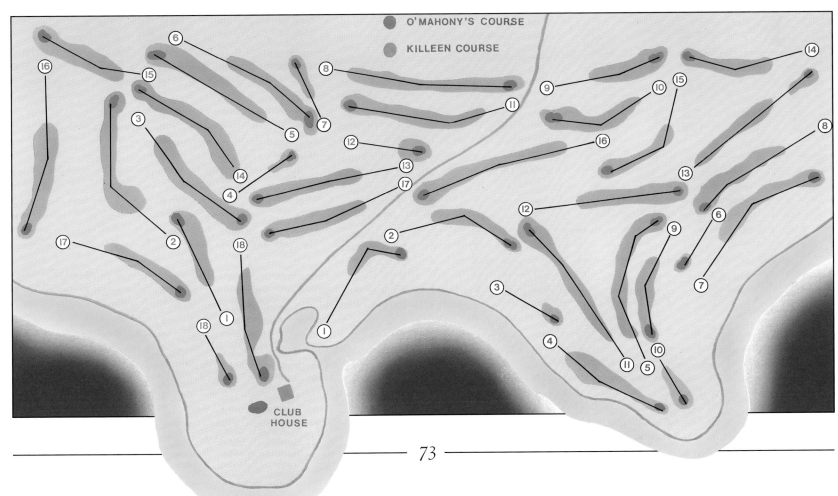

But then, the name of the club is the Killarney Golf and Fishing Club, and Lough Leane does offer splendid fishing facilities!

Killarney's association with the colourful blaze of flowering rhododendrons was planned in 1939. Horticulturalists were instructed to savour the delights of the Augusta club at US Masters time, when golfing buff Lord Castlerosse provided the grounds for the building of a golf course.

1

2

1 *The imposing entrance hall to the new, million-pound clubhouse.*
2 *The clubhouse lounge, offering a splendid view of Killeen's 18th hole.*
3 *An t'Oileán, number 6 feature par three on the Killeen course.*
4 *The 6th green, a raised island, is fraught with danger.*
5 *Home in sight – looking down the 18th fairway to the clubhouse.*

3

4

5

LAHINCH GOLF CLUB
~ OLD COURSE ~ YARDS: 6,735 ~ PAR: 72 ~
~ CASTLE ~ YARDS: 5,236 ~ PAR: 67 ~

A story told about the ready availability of the village butcher to oblige a visitor by presenting himself on the first tee at a moment's notice goes some way to explaining why Lahinch is widely regarded as the St Andrews of Ireland.

Legend has it that when the grateful, though bemused visitor expressed the opinion that if the butcher was prepared to close shop at the prospect of a game of golf, he could hardly make himself much money, 'Maybe not, but he sure makes lots of friends' was the reply, in a telling statement

Location:	Lahinch village
Type:	links
Club administrator:	Alan Reardon (065-81003)
Club professional:	Robert McCavery (065-81408)
Best day for visitors:	welcome every day, booking advisable, championship course

that underlines the sense of occasion at this hotbed of golf.

What strikes you most about the tiny seaside village amid the spectacular scenery of West Clare is that everyone is consciously aware of the historical importance of golf. The special atmosphere manifests itself as you stroll around meeting the local people, whether in their tweed and souvenir shops or in the pubs, playing their traditional music.

This special flavour is prevalent during big competition times, most notably during the traditional July staging of the South of Ireland Amateur Open Championship, the oldest of the provincial championship and in existence since 1895.

The ambience is in keeping with the virtues expressed by Dr Alister MacKenzie when he was called upon to advise on improvements to the original layout, the work of Old Tom Morris, a man also synonymous with the Home of Golf. 'How frequently have I persuaded patients who were

1 Outline challenge of a world-famous par-three attraction, where the green is hidden from view of the teeing ground (2), only to be found beyond the whitewashed stone (3) atop the hill guarding the entrance to the green!
4 Lahinch in times past.
5 The goats of Lahinch (see main text).

	METRES				Index
No.	Blue	White	Green	Par	
1	352	343	328	4	4
2	468	455	438	5	14
3	138	135	128	3	16
4	391	380	372	4	2
5	441	435	430	5	12
6	142	137	127	3	18
7	365	350	339	4	6
8	320	318	309	4	10
9	351	322	313	4	8
Out	2968	2875	2784	36	
10	412	385	375	4	3
11	126	122	116	3	17
12	434	418	400	4	1
13	250	244	234	4	11
14	446	440	435	5	13
15	422	403	395	4	5
16	178	164	150	3	15
17	400	382	382	4	7
18	487	457	450	5	9
In	3155	3015	2937	36	
Tot	6123	5890	5721	72	
SS	73	71	70		

1 The green of the par-three
11th, nestled amid the dunes.
2 Lahinch challenge – since
1914.
3 The clubhouse barometer –
scientific alternative to the goats!
4 Driving over the dunes at the 7th.

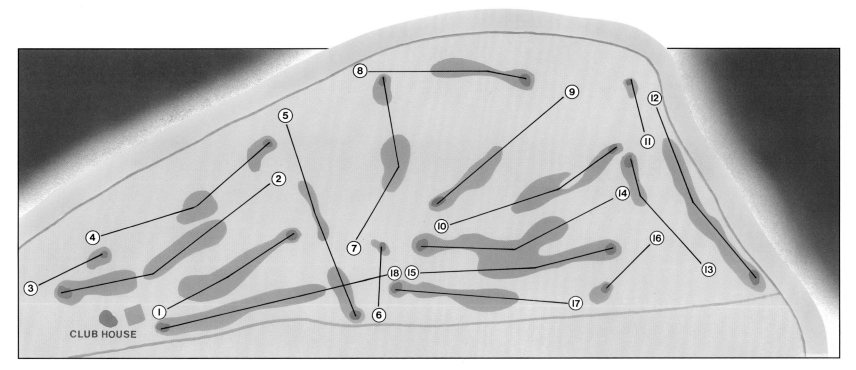

never off my doorstep to take up golf and how rarely, if ever, have I seen them in my consulting rooms after,' said the good doctor, who quit a medical practice to pursue a passion for building golf courses.

MacKenzie acquitted himself admirably at Lahinch, though aspects of the course to this day defy modern architectural trends. Take the infamous Klondyke and Dell holes. It would, of course, be sacrilege to tamper with them, as their curiosity level is such that thousands flock to see for themselves one of the strangest enduring legends of the game.

The 5th hole, the Klondyke, a par five of around 485 yards, sets out on an elevated tee above the craggy beach-side at war with the Atlantic. It demands that the drive be aimed to a narrow alley. The second (or more!) shot then has to be aimed totally blind, over an outrageous mound straddling the fairway. Adding to the intrigue is the fact that the 18th fairway crosses at the other side of the towering mound, and your scorecard carries a warning in bold type that the Lahinch club will not be responsible for any injury caused.

The Dell, the devilish 156-yards par-three 6th, comes next. But where is it, you will ask incredulously? Believe it or not, it is behind that hill in front of you. The whitewashed stone atop the mound is the indicator of the placement of the hole on the other side, so long as the greenkeeper has remembered to move the stone on the day you play!

It is unique and it is Lahinch. You will be all the better for an experience tracing its origins, so the history-conscious locals will tell you, to the time 'when the sleepy village awakened on Good Friday 1893 to the sound of horses, clothed in white foam, making a dramatic entrance as they thundered down the main street, a carriage load of Black Watch officers arriving from the Limerick garrison – and Lahinch golf was under way.'

5 The rolling parallel 12th and 13th holes, with views to the historic castle on the adjoining course, endorse the sentiments of Old Tom Morris that, 'The links is as fine a natural course as has been my good fortune to play over.'

Maximum utilisation of the natural contours of the treasured piece of pure links land is the heart and soul of the course. Clever bunkering is another key element in a challenge dictated not by power but by subtlety.

The 5th and 6th holes aside, the very essence of Lahinch is captured in the thrilling up hill, down dale 4th hole, and things are much the same at the 7th, both approach shots needing to be hit straight into the scenically distracting backdrop of the sea. The 11th hole of only 140 yards is a little gem, and so too is the 13th.

By modern standards the 13th, the Mine, is ridiculously short at 275 yards off the championship tee. To be complacent, however, is to rue for ever the inherent dangers as presented by the 'mine', a deep chasm short right of the two-tiered green, protected by liberal sand. A birdie chance, maybe, but you'll probably end up being thankful for your par – if you can get it.

'Savage as a tiger when the wind blows, mild and lovely on a sunny, calm day,' was the accurate description of the great John Burke. He carved his own special place in the history of the club as the eleven-times winner of the South title. Such was his dominance between 1928 and 1946 that he was often asked not to enter, because other competitors were discouraged by his monopoly, a consequence of which was that the championship and its spin-off connotations for local village business were suffering!

1

2

3

1 *Atlantic Ocean view across to neighbouring Liscannor Harbour.*
2 *Golf Links Hotel and its splendid drawing room (3) in another era.*
4 *The welcoming Lahinch clubhouse today.*
5 *Driving from the 7th green in times long past.*

6 *The neighbouring Cliffs of Moher.*
Ah! Seaweed smells from sandy caves
And thyme and mist in whiffs.
In-coming tide, Atlantic waves
Slapping the sunny cliffs.
Larks' song and sea sounds in the air
And splendour, splendour
everywhere.
                    Sir John Betjeman.

4

5

One of Ireland's great golfing legends concerns the goats at Lahinch.

The story is that a local farmer was given the right to let his goats roam the course, and they tended to collect in the area of the clubhouse whenever the weather was bad. One day, the then secretary, Brud Slattery, attempting to fix the broken clubhouse barometer, in frustration wrote 'See Goats' across its dial, meaning that if the goats were around the clubhouse the weather was likely to be bad, and if they were out and about the course, then you would not require your umbrella! The barometer still hangs in the clubhouse porch.

6

MALONE GOLF CLUB

~ *YARDS: 6,642 ~ PAR: 71* ~

In any 19th-hole discussion attempting to determine the accolade of supreme inland course in Ireland, it is perfectly understandable that there will be a case for the claims of Malone Golf Club. Not much argument is really required for, truth to tell, the gently rolling summertime tapestry of mature wood, restful lake and blaze of flowers sets it quite apart.

Malone's restorative effect is all the more sustaining when you take into account that this tranquil hideaway is a mere four miles outside the troubled city of Belfast!

The fortunate 1,000-plus members made it a permanent case of fourth time lucky when they discovered the delights of the greenbelt Ballydrain Estate in 1962. In search of such a blissful location, bounded by the River Lagan and the Belfast to Drumbeg road, they had attempted three other places, including a polo ground, since the club's formation in 1895.

Set in an attractive parkland of 270 acres, the centrepiece is a beautiful lake of some 25 acres. It is stocked regularly with trout and the like in order to satisfy the sporting needs of the fishing club's members, although the

Location: four miles south of Belfast city

Type: parkland

Club administrator:
Nick Agate (01232-612758)

Club professional:
Michael McGee (01232-614917)

Best day for visitors:
avoid Wednesdays

lake's eagerly sought bounty has at times caused irate officers to line the perimeter with prohibitive barbed wire as a deterrent to nocturnal poachers! Surprisingly, the original layout failed to take account of the water as a core aspect. That oversight has duly been corrected, as you may find to your cost.

On the more trying back nine, you will instinctively find yourself gripping the club more tensely, taking account of a drive over the water at the 13th, and again with the more delicate tee shot required at the exquisite 136-yards 15th. Augusta-like, the green is fiendishly cut into the lake.

1-2 Augusta-like, the green at the feature par-three 15th is cut into part of the 25 acres of trout-filled lake that forms a centrepiece to the wooded, 270-acre Ballydrain greenbelt estate.

1

	Yards	Par	Str
1	382	4	5
2	508	5	17
3	530	5	15
4	160	3	11
5	448	4	3
6	189	3	9
7	470	4	1
8	370	4	13
9	370	4	7
Out	3427	36	
10	410	4	8
11	383	4	10
12	195	3	12
13	403	4	6
14	418	4	2
15	136	3	16
16	312	4	18
17	530	5	14
18	428	4	4
In	3215	35	
Out	3427	36	
Total	6642	71	
SSS	Medal 71		

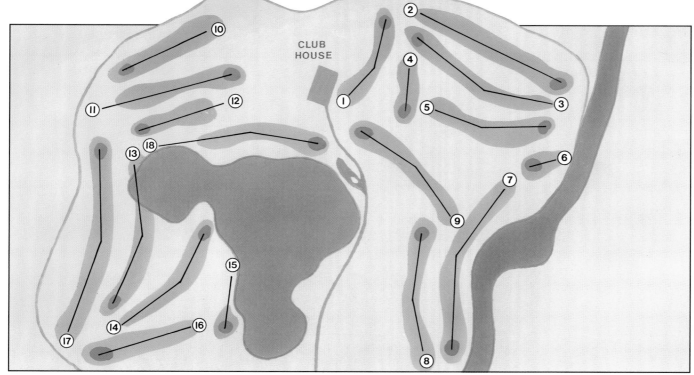

1-2 Golfers beware of other 'hidden' players on the 5th hole. Sound the bell when proceeding!

3 The raised green at the dramatic climax of the par-five 3rd hole which, at 530 yards, joins the 17th as the 'monster' distance challenges at Malone.

4 Malone's mountain ash in bloom.

5 A classic example of Malone's challenging lakeside setting.

6 'Poachers Out' – a stern notice to non members!

5

If you are still in control after all this, the knuckles might have cause to discolour once more with the frightening prospect of the lake to be carried off the 18th tee, and still to be avoided until you hit the sanctuary of the green – hopefully with the same ball.

For its widespread reputation the Malone course does not depend only on the influence of the lake. Trees are Malone's plus mark, and never more so than at the tough, 470-yards dog-leg 7th. It is dominated by giant sycamores.

6

A strict jacket-and-tie ruling applies within an austere old stone clubhouse building, which dates back to around 1835.

The great Tony Jacklin is among the notables you will hear singing the praises of Malone. In the early days at Ballydrain the emerging Malone club hosted the Blaxnit Tournament, and it was here, in 1966, that the man who was to win the British Open in 1969 and the US Open in 1970, and who was later to marry a Belfast woman, won his first important professional title.

MT. JULIET HOTEL AND CLUB
~ YARDS: 7,142 ~ PAR: 72 ~

An exciting new era dawned in Ireland when Jack Nicklaus came to create the Mount Juliet Golf and Country Club at lovely Thomastown in County Kilkenny. The air of expectancy was all the greater as it was his first such architectural undertaking in the country.

A résumé of the Nicklaus curriculum vitae as a designer necessitates consideration of such heralded courses as his beloved Muirfield Village in Dublin, Ohio; the PGA National in Palm Beach Gardens, Florida;

Location:	nine miles from Kilkenny town
Type:	parkland
Club administrator:	Katherine MacCann (056-24455)
Club Professional:	Leadbetter Academy (056 -24455)
Best day for visitors:	ring for appointment

Grand Cypress in Orlando; the Glen Abbey Club in Toronto and the Australian Club in Sydney, Australia.

Rest assured that Mount Juliet is good enough to consolidate the sequence and to be presented as proof positive that, while Nicklaus the golfer is legend, Nicklaus the designer will similarly be immortalised.

Golf at Mount Juliet is the jewel in the crown. The 18-hole championship course is the centrepiece of a new concept in Ireland, similar to the Kildare Hotel and Country

1 *The period 18th-century hotel exudes warmth and personality.*
2 *'And peace comes dropping slow' – Mount Juliet's restful drawingroom.*
3 *The graciousness of the hotel's Lady Helen restaurant.*
4 *The awesome lake carry to the green at the showpiece par-three 3rd.*
5 *Club favourite – the Irish wolfhound 'Warlock'.*

4

5

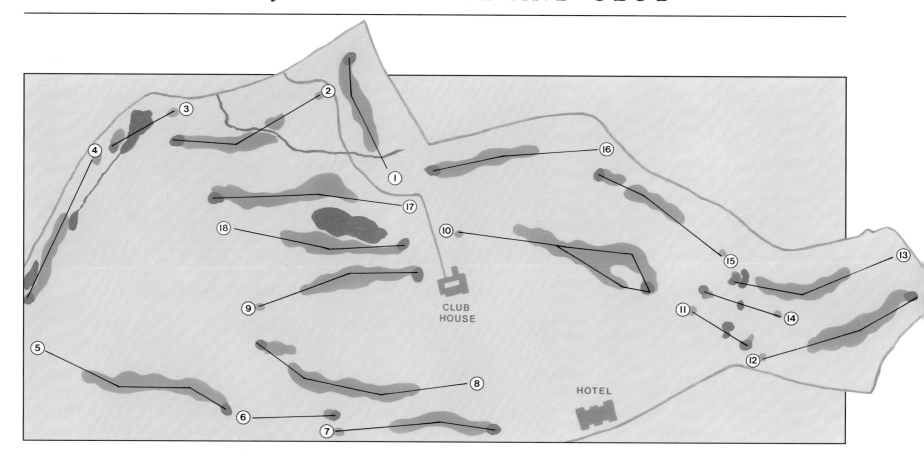

1

1 *More water to negotiate on the narrow entrance to the 4th green.*
2 *Undulating ground and a brook are features of the setting for the par-three 11th.*

3-4 *'Building a golf course is my total expression,' said designer Jack Nicklaus. The view from the 17th tee (3) and the approach to the 18th green (4), illustrate his sentiment.*
5 *Pheasant galore in a sporting environment.*

Club. Luxury resort golf has been unveiled for the first time in a package embracing a multiplicity of pursuits, built around the tranquillity of the imposing 18th-century mansion, now converted into a luxury hotel. Set in 1,500 acres of invigorating woodlands encircling the River Nore, the offer is also to come and fish the well-stocked river, enjoy shooting at a clay target academy, indulge in a spot of archery, or horse ride along the secluded, ambling trekking trails of one of Ireland's largest and most beautiful walled estates, dating back to the 17th century.

By the highest standards, the layout meets all the promises made by the designer when he first explored the rich pasturelands and exclaimed: 'I think Mount Juliet gets high marks ... it's just a beautiful piece of property on which to build a golf course.'

What strikes you forcefully is the design concept. The long-established pilgrim spots in Ireland, such as Portmarnock, Ballybunnion, Royal Portrush, Royal County Down etc., have always ensured Ireland's high pedigree. As architectural trends and general standards change, however, the advent of Mount Juliet puts Irish golf in a new class.

Earmarked as a prospective venue for the staging of the Irish Open Championship,

2

3

5

the vast expanse of gently rolling country-side has been custom-built for such an eventuality, and Nicklaus's canny design concept has also taken account of the needs of spectators. Thus it can be said that Mount Juliet is Ireland's first purpose-built, mounded spectator course.

It is also true to state that playing Mount Juliet is to experience the delights of an American-type course. Artistically shaped fairways, destructively created bunkers, tantalisingly contoured greens ... and, in true American fashion, water is seen to play an integral part.

Guaranteed to scare the life out of you is the all-carry par-three 3rd hole of almost 200 yards – over water! On the awesome back nine, the little 11th is a skilful short pitch over the same stretch of water that you will encounter on the way back to another marvellous feature hole, the 13th.

4

No.	Metres			Par	Index
	Blue	White	Green		
1	332	313	296	4	17
2	379	352	319	4	10
3	168	154	128	3	15
4	368	351	312	4	1
5	488	465	442	5	14
6	209	183	173	3	7
7	381	351	319	4	9
8	528	504	481	5	4
9	388	351	341	4	8
Out	3241	3024	2811	36	
10	499	474	451	5	5
11	154	127	100	3	18
12	381	359	332	4	11
13	399	377	352	4	3
14	180	162	143	3	6
15	339	320	300	4	16
16	396	372	340	4	13
17	471	450	435	5	12
18	433	408	380	4	2
In	3252	3049	2833	36	
Tot	6493	6073	5644	72	

And still there is no reprieve, as a huge lake separates the 17th and 18th fairways, so that a par-five, par-four finish is enough to convince you (momentarily, of course) that you are actually as good as Jack Nicklaus himself.

'Building a golf course is my total expression. My golf game can only go on so long. But what I have learned can be put into a piece of ground to last beyond me.' This is the Jack Nicklaus philosophy that convinced wealthy businessman Tim 'Toyota' Mahony that the Golden Bear was the man to create his dream course.

MULLINGAR GOLF CLUB

~ YARDS: 6,370 ~ PAR: 72 ~

Friendships made at Mullingar are lasting' is a fond sentiment you will hear echoed the world over, because prominent among the club's many virtues is the warmth of the welcome. *Céad Míle Fáilte* might well be the club's motto, as down through the ages successive generations of members have steadfastly perpetuated the honourable sentiment. Is it any wonder that the top-rated parkland course is so favourably viewed, and by so many?

The success of the annual August Bank Holiday Open Scratch Trophy compounds the point. It is a major 72-holes amateur championship, in which successful professionals like Des Smyth, Peter Townsend, John O'Leary, Ronan Rafferty and Philip Walton first cut their competitive teeth. It is also an event synonymous with amateur legends such as Joe Carr, Tom Craddock, Rodney Foster, Mark Gannon and Martin O'Brien.

The professionals, too, have many times graced the lovely fairways in their serene setting on the Belvedere Demesne, amid some famed old oak and in a haven where

Location:
three miles south of Mullingar town
Type: parkland
Club administrator:
Brian Kiely (044-48366)
Club professional:
John Burns (044-40085)
Best day for visitors:
avoid Wednesdays and weekends

the player is ever conscious of respite from the madding crowd.

Ever since envied championship status was accorded in 1952, when the club staged the Irish Professional Championship, the story of how the pros fared on James Braid's magnificent creation has provided fascinating recall.

In 1952, Fred Daly mustered the unlikely finish of birdie, par, eagle to beat his old playing partner Harry Bradshaw; Norman Drew, the first Irishman ever to play in the Walker Cup, Ryder Cup and World (Canada) Cup, won when the championship returned

1 An autumnal view of Mullingar's beautiful parkland setting.
2 The renowned green at the 2nd hole, a James Braid masterpiece. Guarded by sand and streams, it has been voted one of the best in Ireland.

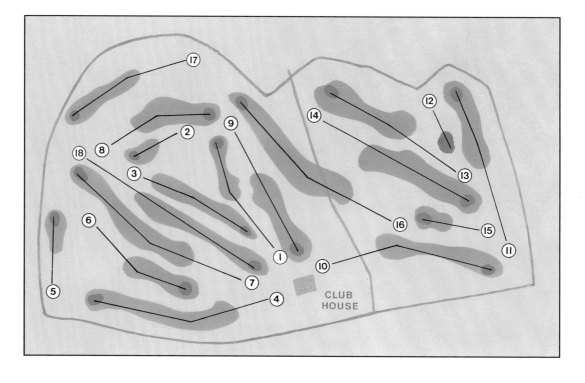

in 1959; Christy O'Connor Snr, a man who always held the Mullingar course close to his heart, triumphed in another Irish Championship in 1965; and to maintain the tradition of players with only the very best pedigree rising to the top at Mullingar, the popular Paddy Skerritt was the winner when the Irish Match Play Championship was staged in 1970.

Mullingar is quite rightly recognised as one of James Braid's best architectural efforts. His eagle eye spotted the potential instantly. No sooner had the former British Open champion completed his initial reconnaissance mission of 'blasted heath, gorse and scrub' in 1937 than the far-seeing old Scot with the distinctive walrus moustache asked for a hatchet and three dozen wooden pegs!

Then, the story goes, before the Committee members' startled eyes, Braid stood back into the middle of the gorse and, with fitting perception of the practical as well as the picturesque, carved his master-piece as he pegged off 18 tees and 18 greens,

1

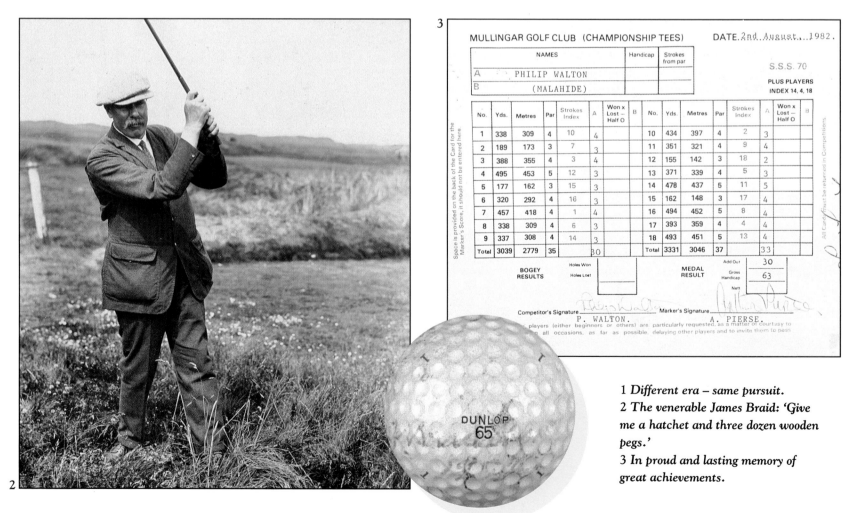

3

MULLINGAR GOLF CLUB (CHAMPIONSHIP TEES)										DATE 2nd August 1982.				
NAMES				Handicap	Strokes from par					S.S.S. 70				
A	PHILIP WALTON													
B	(MALAHIDE)									PLUS PLAYERS INDEX 14, 4, 18				
No.	Yds.	Metres	Par	Strokes Index	A	Won x Lost – Half O	B	No.	Yds.	Metres	Par	Strokes Index	A	B
1	338	309	4	10	4			10	434	397	4	2	3	
2	189	173	3	7	3			11	351	321	4	9	4	
3	388	355	4	3	4			12	155	142	3	18	2	
4	495	453	5	12	3			13	371	339	4	5	3	
5	177	162	3	15	3			14	478	437	5	11	5	
6	320	292	4	16	3			15	162	148	3	17	4	
7	457	418	4	1	4			16	494	452	5	8	4	
8	338	309	4	6	3			17	393	359	4	4	4	
9	337	308	4	14	3			18	493	451	5	13	4	
Total	3039	2779	35		30			Total	3331	3046	37		33	

BOGEY RESULTS	Holes Won		MEDAL RESULT	Add Out	30
	Holes Lost			Gross Handicap	63
				Nett	

Competitor's Signature _____ Marker's Signature _____

P. WALTON. A. PIERSE.

n players (either beginners or others) are particularly requested, as a matter of courtesy to
n all occasions, as far as possible, delaying other players and to invite them to pass.

DUNLOP
65

1 *Different era – same pursuit.*
2 *The venerable James Braid: 'Give me a hatchet and three dozen wooden pegs.'*
3 *In proud and lasting memory of great achievements.*

2

the hospitable 19th, which has the additional appeal of commanding good views of at least seven holes.

Individuality is the key to the layout of the holes. There is, therefore, a wide variety from which to choose a favourite, although the opinion is that if you can get your par three at the 198-yards second hole, where you are hitting a lot of club from a high teeing area to a highly perched green, fronted by a ditch and guarded by bunkers, then you are already on your way to a good score.

The favourable disposition of the legendary Christy O'Connor Snr to the Mullingar course is best illustrated by his comments on the infamous dog leg, par five 16th hole. The most spectacular and maybe controversial design by James Braid, the hole is noted for the open ditch that runs across the fairway, precisely at the point of the dog leg.

Says Christy, 'It is peculiar how magnetic a hazard like this can be. The man who tries too hard to keep out of it is likely to find that this is the easiest way to get into it!'

pocketed his fee of £25, caught the train to Dublin, and thence the mail boat to take him home to Scotland.

That virtuoso effort was duly complemented by the strategic positioning of the clubhouse (lately given a huge facelift), so that three greens – the 3rd, 9th and 18th – have the effect of a semi-arc around

4 Belvedere Demesne setting amid famed old oak trees.
5 'Hazardous' approach to the hospitable clubhouse, one of Ireland's favourite 19th holes.
6 Mullingar's serene setting, where friendships once made are lasting!

PORTMARNOCK GOLF CLUB
~ *YARDS: 7,136 ~ PAR: 72* ~

Providence intended Portmarnock to be a golf course and, thanks to the vision of Pickeman and Ross, man has improved on that providence.

Reverently regarded as the golfing equivalent of a National heritage, for the chance discovery of the Republic of Ireland's premier course we can be grateful to the intrepid Messrs W.C. Pickeman and George Ross, for it was their curiosity about the potential of the rugged span jutting out into Dublin Bay that inspired them to row their boat across from the mainland.

That bit of history was enacted in 1889, and it was due to the enthusiasm of this intrepid pair, notwithstanding the blessing of the landlord, the whiskey distiller Jameson, that Portmarnock's first clubhouse was formally opened on St Stephen's Day in 1894.

Ross was called upon to strike the opening shot on the new course, and it is a measure of the appreciative Portmarnock club membership that the hickory stick with which he made his historic stroke survives as a treasured memento in their imposing and artistic clubhouse.

By any standards Portmarnock is one of the foremost golf clubs in the world. The staging of the first sell-out and live televised

1 View of the first green looking back towards the clubhouse and estuary.
2 Clubhouse wall Ship's Bell, in use until 1922. It tolled to signal the departure of the last boat across the estuary to the mainland.

Location: six miles north-east of Dublin city
Type: links
Club administrator: John Quigley (01-8462968)
Club professional: Joey Purcell (01-8462634)
Best day for visitors: avoid weekends and public holidays

2

Walker Cup match, in 1991, maintained a proud club tradition of successfully hosted amateur (British amateur in 1949) and professional (Dunlop Masters, 1959 and 1965; Alcan Golfer of the Year 1970; World

(Canada) Cup 1960) championships. Now there is talk that the Ryder Cup could follow to this venue voted by the players of the European PGA Tour as the best they visit.

The 1959 Masters is documented as one of the greatest events. It is fondly recalled as the occasion when Christy O'Connor Snr, with a final round of 66, wiped out Joe Carr's four-shot lead and so prevented the famous amateur, the son of the Portmarnock club steward, from pegging the professionals. Also recorded in history is the fact that the success of the World (Canada) Cup in 1960 was responsible for the ensuing growth of interest in golf in Ireland.

The long-established tradition of Portmarnock as an ideal championship links finds its roots in the story of the Irish Open. Concerned members, desperate to keep the good image of Ireland in the golfing shop-window, dug deep into their own pockets and unselfishly came up with the money to finance the staging of the inaugural tournament in 1927. The winner, George Duncan, lining his body with brown paper as insulation against the wind and rain, earned the princely sum of £160!

Ever since that time Portmarnock endures as the spiritual home of Ireland's biggest and best international sporting occasion, whilst sharing the actual staging of the Open with other clubs.

Grateful Irish golf fans have, therefore, been able to thrill to the exploits of Ballesteros, Faldo, Player, Trevino, Norman, Weis-

kopf, and Lyle, the latter somehow managing to plunder a new course record 64 in 1989. The figure of 65 had stood for 30 years!

Tom Watson, on a private visit, wondered why the links was not on the British Open rota, a sentiment also expressed many long years ago by the South African Bobby Locke as he was winning the Irish Open title of 1938.

The late Harry Bradshaw, the loveable resident pro here for almost 40 years, always contended that Portmarnock's greatest quality was that 'it is a fair course.'

The fine eye of the club's first professional, Mungo Park, brother of the more renowned Willie and, of course, son of Willie Snr, winner of the first British Open Championship in 1860, gave a helping hand in the cleverly varied design. No two consecutive holes are laid in the same direction, thereby putting the golfer at the whim of the Irish Sea breezes from Ireland's Eye, or around from Howth Head.

In an era when power hitting has defused much of the difficulty of hickory-

1 *Portmarnock Club's opening day, 1894, play on the 15th hole. John Petrie, about to hit, watched by founder member and first Captain George Ross (extreme left).*
2 *Low-tide pony and trap access across the estuary to the course.*
3 *Humble origins: the first clubhouse.*

HOLE	METRES			PAR	S.I.
	Blue	White	Green		
1	358	346	325	4	13
2	346	322	312	4	15
3	351	348	339	4	11
4	407	401	395	4	1
5	364	355	345	4	5
6	550	530	520	5	9
7	161	144	129	3	17
8	368	351	336	4	7
9	404	386	361	4	3
	3309	3183	3062	36	
10	341	333	323	4	8
11	389	382	372	4	2
12	136	126	116	3	18
13	516	502	492	5	14
14	359	352	342	4	6
15	191	181	171	3	12
16	484	469	457	5	16
17	423	394	376	4	4
18	381	364	354	4	10
	3220	3103	3003	36	

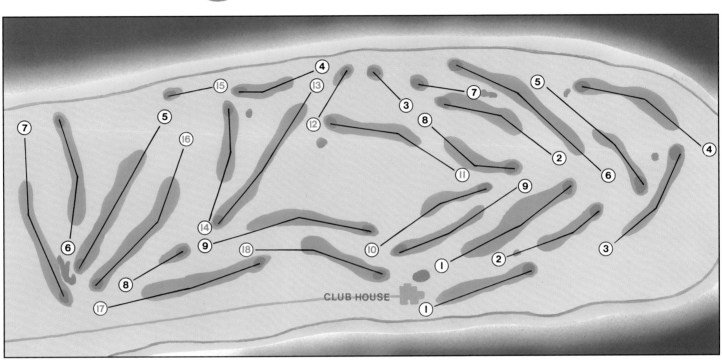

4 Antique putter presented in 1978 by Dr P.J. Hillery, President of Ireland, which hangs in the Members' Bar and is played for in foursome competitions.
5 Flowering lily pond close by the 4th green.

shafted times gone by, the classically traditional Portmarnock stands up to any examination. The awesome proportions of the finishing stretch stand honourable guard and, even if you emerge from the shortish par-four 14th (393 yards), of great notoriety and classic design, and then from the infamous par-three 15th, by the intimidating sea shore close by scenic Ireland's Eye, fairly well intact, you are still made to run the gauntlet of the ultimate golfing experience over the finishing three holes.

One of the best-known symbols among the memorabilia lovingly collected at Portmarnock is the Ship's Bell. It hangs on the clubhouse gable wall, close by the first tee and at a point where the original approach to the course was across the estuary by boat, or at low tide by horse and cart. Presented to the club by a Captain Weatherall in 1909, the bell was tolled to signal the departure of the last boat back to the mainland, and was in use until 1922, when the boat was replaced by the increasingly popular motor-car.

Ben Crenshaw, the 1984 US Masters champion, while winning the Irish Open in 1976 so enjoyed playing the course that he said he would love to take the 15th hole back home to America! In a survey conducted in 1990, Nick Faldo and Greg Norman also named Portmarnock's 185-yard par three 15th hole in their 'Best in the World' category.

1 **Hard by Dublin Bay, the celebrated par-three 15th, lovingly described by US Masters champion Ben Crenshaw as 'one of the greatest short holes on earth'.**
2 **Scenic Ireland's Eye is the line for the equally acclaimed par-four 14th hole.**
3 **Portmarnock's clubhouse.**

4 Enchanting sunset setting for just one more hole ....

5 The 4th green in grassy surrounds, a reminder of times past, when inhabitants of the peninsula on which the links stands indulged in illicit moonshining. Rye was grown and the locals were none too pleased when visiting golfers tramped through the cornfield in search of lost balls!

PORTMARNOCK HOTEL AND GOLF LINKS

~ YARDS: 6,877 ~ PAR: 71 ~

The emergence of Portmarnock Hotel and Golf Links as one of Ireland's premier new places to play epitomises the better virtues of Ireland's golfing boom. Situated on the shoreline of the peninsula jutting out into the Irish Sea and an immediate neighbour to the long-standing Portmarnock Golf Club, it combines the facilities of a luxury hotel with the quite awesome discovery of a new links.

Considering that less than one per cent of all courses in Europe are of genuine links stock, you can readily appreciate the esteem associated with the advent of a complex strategically located only 15 minutes from Dublin Airport and 25 minutes from Dublin city centre.

The Portmarnock Hotel and Golf Links is unusual in Ireland in that there are no members! The golf course is designed 'to encourage visitors from overseas to sample the golfing delights in Ireland'.

The location, combined with the on-site hotel facility and quality of course, understandably makes it one of the most sought after places to play.

A fascinating backdrop to this latest jewel in Ireland's necklace of great links venues is its deep-rooted sense of history. The opening tee shot is negotiated hard by a graveyard and final resting place of St Marnock. Little could he have foreseen when he established his monastery on the site that his name would be dedicated to the Mecca of golf now synonymous with the locality.

Location: 11 miles east of Dublin city

Type: links

Club administrator:
Moira Cassidy (01-8460611)

Best day for visitors:
visitors welcome

Hole	Ch'ship	Medal	Par	S.I.
1	389	352	4	14
2	396	385	4	10
3	195	189	3	12
4	579	561	5	6
5	474	449	4	2
6	534	508	5	18
7	453	445	4	4
8	376	355	4	8
9	171	152	3	16
10	532	513	5	15
11	460	446	4	1
12	361	347	4	5
13	150	148	3	17
14	348	343	4	13
15	400	387	4	7
16	408	389	4	11
17	203	188	3	9
18	448	406	4	3
Total	6,877	6,563	71	

• *all distances in yards*

1 A blend of elegance and good taste – the 18th hole with superb clubhouse and hotel beyond.
2 The tantalising par-three 9th – the only hole on the links without a bunker.

Perhaps that ecclesiastical association inspired one awe-struck golfer, after he had played the links, to proclaim: 'when God was making the world he laid out the dunes and terrain so that one day a great golf links would be sited here'.

The renowned Bernhard Langer takes credit for the embroidery! His design and layout brushwork is notable for the fact that he manages the quite uncanny blend of the traditional perspective with all that is best in modern architectural trends.

If there is a sense of reprieve in the playing of some early holes, the sting in the tail is the challenge that quickly unfolds and endures to the death. Arrival at the spectacular dunes side of the links heralds a sequence of quite fabulous holes in classic links terrain.

The truly delightful par-four 8th hole, dog-legging left with the green tucked amid the sandhills, establishes the tone. From that juncture, it is a riveting case of one hole being better than the preceding one and the finishing three being better than most!

From a high-pitched tee hard by the seashore, the 150 yards carry off the 16th traverses an intimidating, deep hollow. No. 17 is a dramatic uphill par-three with a cavernous bunker fronting the green and where local lore holds that 'birdies are rare, par is to be treasured and bogies are all too plentiful!'

The masterpiece is completed when you are confronted with the tight drive out of the dunes at the 18th and then head right to where the green is nestled in a natural amphitheatre in the shadow of the imposing Portmarnock Hotel. It is an impressive and welcoming backdrop.

The land upon which the hotel and links is situated once belonged to the Jameson family of Irish whiskey fame. The former Jameson family home has been redeveloped into a hotel, which overlooks the course.

2

The beach adjoining the links witnessed the daring exploits of pioneering aviators. On August 18th, 1932, Mr James Mollison, husband of Amy Johnson, took off on a solo flight in his Puss Moth 'The Heart's Content'. It is acknowledged as the first solo east-to-west crossing of the Atlantic.

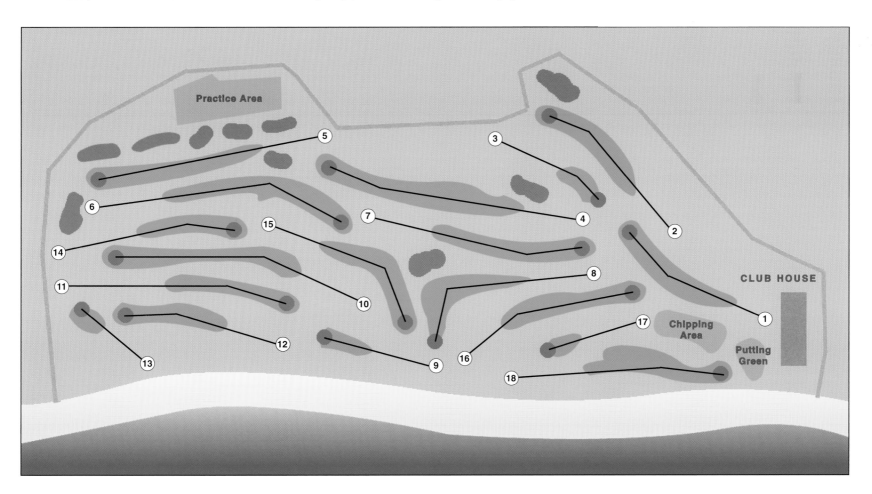

1

3

PORTSTEWART GOLF CLUB
~ YARDS: 6,784 ~ PAR: 72 ~

Down through the ages, the boast at Portstewart Golf Club has been that it possesses, quite simply, 'the finest opening hole in the game'. There is hardly a person of golfing soul who would disagree.

To confine the commendation only to the breathtaking opener, where the tee shot is hit deep down into an amphitheatre amid the sandy dunes that appealingly set the overall mood, is, nonetheless, vastly to underestimate the all-embracing pleasure of golf at one of the most frequented holiday resorts in Ireland.

The pleasure has now been enhanced as a consequence of an adventurous decision by the members to purchase additional land, known as Thistly Hollow, from the National Trust, which has resulted in seven

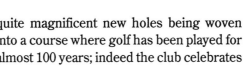

Location:
one mile from town centre

Club administrator:
Michael Moss (01265-832015)

Club professional:
Alan Hunter (01265-832601)

Best day for visitors:
avoid weekends

quite magnificent new holes being woven into a course where golf has been played for almost 100 years; indeed the club celebrates its Centenary Year in 1994.

It also means that Portstewart, at its strand course, has 27 holes: the 'Blue' nine incorporating the weaker holes of the original course, with the 18-hole Town Course close by.

Little wonder, therefore, that the club feels it is fast emerging from the shadows of its more lauded Royal Portrush neighbour.

The sense of satisfaction is all the greater because the newly acquired land of towering, rolling dunes and undulating valleys comprising 60 acres of 'God's own country' was purchased in 1981 for a mere £17,500.

Immediately after the acclaimed first hole, you climb into the new territory, where the elevation offers panoramic views of the golden sweep of Portstewart strand, the busy holiday town across the Atlantic inlet, and of the River Bann.

The natural shape of land has surrendered itself ideally to classic links golf. Elevated tees, rolling valleys, hogs-back contours and subtle dog-legging amid the plentiful buckthorn combine in fascinating splendour and challenge.

1 *Clubhouse facilities complement an outstanding links.*
2 *'God's Own Country'.*
3 *The magnificence of the new holes in Thistly Hollow, viewed from high above the 2nd green.*
4 *The day that Bobby Locke, five times British Open champion, played a qualifying round in 1951.*

MARKER'S SCORE	HOLE No.	METRES	YARDS	PAR	GROSS SCORE
	1	381	417	4	
	2	313	342	4	
	3	353	386	4	
	4	331	362	4	
	5	141	154	3	
	6	448	490	5	
	7	429	475	5	
	8	145	159	3	
	9	367	401	4	
OUT		2908	3186	36	
	10	389	425	4	
	11	162	177	3	
	12	494	540	5	
	13	183	200	3	
	14	447	489	5	
	15	304	333	4	
	16	381	417	4	
	17	374	409	4	
	18	388	424	4	
IN		3122	3414	36	
OUT		2908	3186	36	
TOTAL		6030	6600	72	
HANDICAP					
NET SCORE					

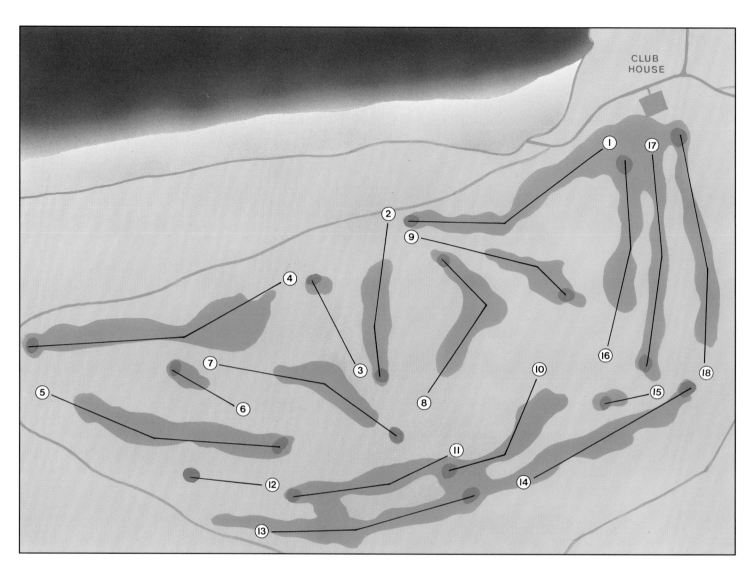

1

2

1 *Third green cul-de-sac setting amid the gorse.*
2 *The River Bann and estuary with the 5th green in the foreground.*
3 *Visitors welcome: Perpetual Trophy for the Causeway Coast tournament.*
4 *Distilling golf – the Black Bush Trophy.*
5 *Humps and hollows make for a testing entrance onto the green at the 386-yard 4th hole.*
6 *For the veterans.*

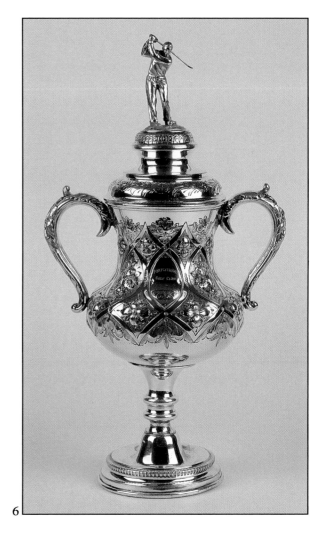

the club members, most notably to course architect (and local schoolteacher) Des Giffin, tireless club secretary-manager Michael Moss, the club professional Alan Hunter, the course manager Bernard Findley, and new course chairman Richard McCorduck, who is also the local bank manager.

The late South African Bobby Locke led the praises of Portstewart as long ago as 1951, when the Old Course was utilised as a

At times it may be prudent to take an iron off the tee. The respectful reminder seems especially appropriate at the 384-yards par-four 8th, described as a 'crescent-shaped dog leg'.

You will thrill, too, to the challenge of the 140-yards par-three 6th. It is billed as Portstewart's own 'Postage Stamp', as at Royal Troon, and it surely is a potential card-wrecker. Miss the green to the right and you are confronted with the onerous task of a

finely cut-up shot from 40 feet below a green into which are cut two forbidding sand traps. If the wind is blowing, you will have to punch a four or five iron to have any hope of a satisfactory result.

In an era of which it is accurately said that the cost of new golf courses is counted in millions, it is interesting to point out that the Portstewart course has been remodelled for under £100,000, irrigation included.

The result is an outstanding tribute to

qualifying round for the British Open Championship, won by Max Faulkner, at Royal Portrush. An equally memorable Irish Amateur Championship was won in 1960 by noted Ulster and Irish international Michael Edwards.

It was fitting that the national amateur championship returned to the club in 1992, thereby allowing a new generation to savour the delights of a reconstructed golf links bearing all the hallmarks of the vintage best.

ROYAL BELFAST GOLF CLUB

~ YARDS: 6,274 ~ PAR: 70 ~

Conjecture may well continue about where precisely golf was first played in Ireland, as much as where the game itself was invented. What is fact, however, is that Royal Belfast is the country's oldest club.

It celebrated its Centenary Year in 1981, being founded on 9 November, 1881, a historic landmark as the inspiration for the growth and organisation of the game in Ireland.

The telling influences in the formation of the formal structuring of the game were of Scottish origin, in that a certain Thomas Sinclair, while holidaying in Scotland, was invited to St Andrews and was at once smitten.

Location:
eight miles north-east of the city

Type: parkland

Club administrator:
Ms Susanna Morrison (01232-428165)

Club professional:
Christopher Spence (01232-428165)

Best day for visitors:
avoid Thursdays and Saturdays

On his return to Belfast he eagerly sought out the Scottish-born Royal Academy schoolteacher George Baillie, who was already a convert to the game from his days in his native Musselburgh. The two like-minded visionaries acted quickly in pursuit of their passion, and in a matter of weeks they had established the Belfast Golf Club on 80 acres of land at the Kinnegar, Holywood.

The club was to assume the Royal prefix within four years, when the Prince of Wales, during a visit to Ireland, was invited

1 Historic account of Kinnegar, birthplace of Royal Belfast in 1881.
2 Craigavad and the shape of one of the finest 18-hole parkland settings in golf.

1

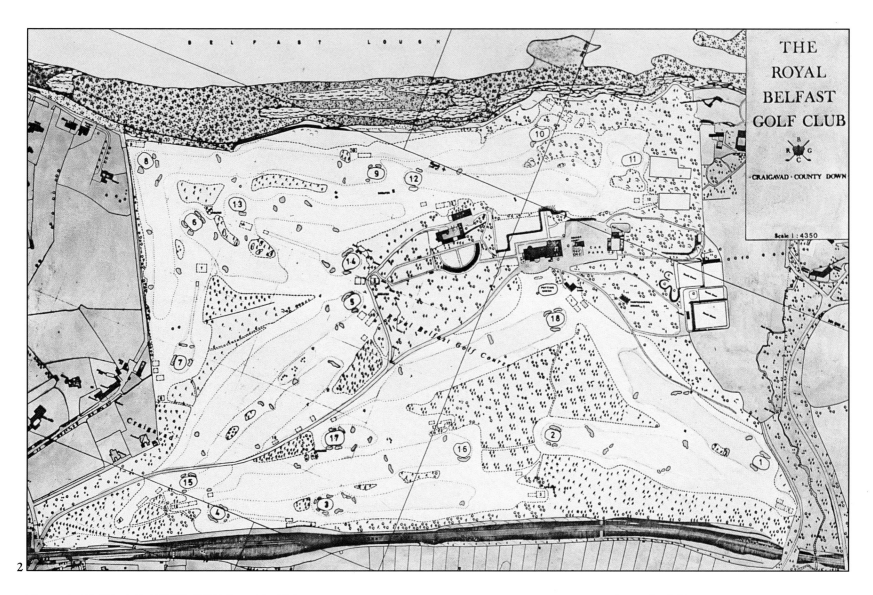

2

3

3 A stately clubhouse, once the residence of Belfast's Lord Mayor.

to become patron. The current patron is Prince Philip, Duke of Edinburgh.

Following those formative years the club moved on to a site in Carnalea, at Bangor, because of increasing numbers wanting to play (by 1890 membership had risen to 160). But when that essentially fun nine-holer was also found to be inadequate the club moved for a third and final time in 1925, when Craigavad House and Demesne became available. It provided the scope for what has subsequently become established as one of the finest 18-hole parkland settings in the game.

Royal Belfast's Victorian ambiance is entirely in keeping with the club's revered position in the game. To start with, the clubhouse was probably the stately home of the Rt Hon. J.C. White, once Lord Mayor of the city. Another distinguishing feature is its serene setting amid trees and colourful foliage. Additional enhancement sees the commodious course fall gently away to the scenic southern shore of Belfast Lough.

1

Heed the wise old golfer's tale, therefore, that the greens tend to fall towards the sea.

In addition to golf, other sports played at the 1,200-member club include tennis and squash rackets.

It is to his eternal credit that H.S. Colt, the eminent English course architect of the day, grasped the full potential of the site. The happy consequence has been that the Royal Belfast Club is in proud possession

2

1 Landmark for Ireland's oldest golf club.
2 A view of the 14th green, falling gently away to the scenic shores of Belfast Lough, supports local advice that putts will tend to fall towards the sea.

3

4

Player Col M H Cork **Competition** ON HIS 81st Birthday

Handicap **Date** 6th Nov 1972

(Standard Scratch Score 70)

Marker's Score	HOLE	Yards	Par	Stroke Index	Score	Marker's Score	HOLE	Yards	Par	Stroke Index	Score
	1	442	4	7	4		10	325	4	10	3
	2	412	4	3	6		11	172	3	14	3
	3	362	4	13	5		12	422	4	2	6
	4	130	3	17	3		13	358	4	12	4
	5	526	5	1	4		14	190	3	16	5
	6	340	4	11	4		15	418	4	4	6
	7	189	3	15	3		16	506	5	6	5
	8	405	4	9	5		17	198	3	18	4
	9	415	4	5	5		18	522	5	8	5
	OUT	3221	35		39		HOME	3111	35		41
							OUT	3221	35		
							TOTAL	6332	70		
							HANDICAP				
							NET SCORE				

Marker's Signature A. J. Lowson

Player's Signature M H Cork

5

6

3 A memento of the club's inauguration meeting, held at Carnalea in June 1893.
4 Shoreside setting for play on the 9th green.
5 Clubhouse artefacts in honour of Col Paddy Cork, who scored lower than his age on the occasion of his 81st birthday!
6 A feathery ball, circa 1820-40, owned by founder member William Johnston and presented to the club by his granddaughter.

of one of the province's beauty spots, into which a collection of fine holes has been set.

At the heart of the varied challenge is the constant requirement of accuracy, rather than length. 'Devious rather than difficult' is how some equate its merits.

David Carson, the club professional, boasts that the very first hole 'is one of the best starting holes in Ulster.' It measures 417 yards from the back tee and is slightly dog leg to the left. That little teaser is then followed by what the pro describes as 'perhaps the most attractive-looking of the 18 holes.'

Straight away, therefore, you can embrace the very heart of the Royal Belfast course, and the sense of anticipation will intensify as you build up to those holes down by the invigorating Lough shore.

1 *'Devious rather than difficult' – the 12th green mirrors the tone.*
2 *Old Inn at neighbouring Crawfordsburn, the oldest in Ireland. Peter the Great of Russia and highwayman Dick Turpin are reputed to have lodged there.*
3 *Tilting landscape of the 9th to 12th fairways.*
4 *How architect H.S. Colt grasped the full potential of a rare site.*

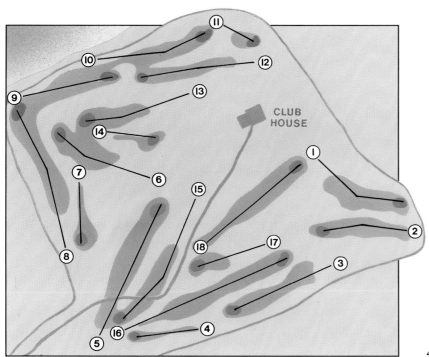

Hole	Yards Blue	Yards White	Yards Green	Par	Stroke Index
1	417	414	409	4	7
2	404	400	395	4	3
3	372	359	354	4	13
4	143	140	135	3	15
5	555	550	487	5	9
6	351	348	340	4	11
7	184	164	160	3	17
8	394	392	360	4	5
9	409	406	400	4	1
OUT	3229	3173	3040	35	
10	303	299	293	4	14
11	165	162	158	3	8
12	433	430	424	4	4
13	360	357	354	4	12
14	187	184	180	3	10
15	410	407	393	4	2
16	485	476	466	5	16
17	193	190	185	3	18
18	509	506	470	5	6
IN	3045	3011	2923	35	
OUT	3229	3173	3040	35	
TOTAL	6274	6184	5963	70	

ROYAL CO. DOWN GOLF CLUB

~ *YARDS: 6,968 ~ PAR: 71* ~

Golf might well have remained a minority sport in Ireland had it not been for a go-ahead railway company official, who exploited the unknown fishing village of Newcastle, Co. Down.

Joseph Tatlow was the enterprising manager of the old Belfast and County Down Railway, and it occurred to him that, since the Belfast Golf Club was proving such a curiosity, another club somewhere along his line would be a big boost for business. Little could he have realised that he was to inspire the creation of a golf club that would attract people to travel from all over the world.

Founded in 1889, the second-oldest club in Northern Ireland has long been revered as one of the world's truly classic links. 'Exhilarating even without a club in your hand,' it was intuitively observed, in respectful recognition of a course essentially laid out by Old Tom Morris and later approved of by Vardon and then by Colt.

According to the early minutes of the club, Morris was adjured not to let his costs exceed four guineas (£4.20p). Considering his artistic expression in such a setting, the present generation is left bewildered by the massive sums of money now expended in the creation of courses.

The links at Newcastle defy you to stand atop the heather-strewn hill over which the drive to the 9th hole is aimed, or by the adjacent 4th tee, and nominate a rival to match the view. Before your eyes are the majestic Mourne Mountains and the peaks of Slieve Donard and Slieve Bearnagh, on a

Location:	half a mile from Newcastle	
Type:	links	
Club administrator:	P.E. Rolph (013967-23314)	
Club professional:	Neil Manchip/Kevin Whitson (01396-722419)	
Best day for visitors:	ring for an appointment	

Hole	CHAMP. Blue	MEDAL White	F'WARD MEDAL Yellow	Par
1	506	500	500	5
2	424	374	374	4
3	473	473	454	4
4	217	217	174	3
5	440	418	409	4
6	396	368	358	4
7	145	129	129	3
8	427	428	424	4
9	(486)	431	431	(5) 4
OUT	3514	3338	3253	35
10	200	200	192	3
11	440	429	429	4
12	501	476	476	5
13	445	422	422	4
14	213	213	202	3
15	445	445	420	4
16	265	265	236	4
17	400	376	376	4
18	545	528	528	5
IN	3454	3354	3281	36
OUT	3514	3338	3253	35
TOTAL	6968	6692	6534	71
S.S.S.	73	72	71	H'cap

line through the spire of the distinctive red-bricked Slieve Donard Hotel. Turning left seaward, behold the sandy expanse of Dundrum Bay reaching out to the lighthouse at St John's Point. This is the traditional view of Newcastle and one of the most photographed in the world.

Set against modern architectural demands, a little of Newcastle would be considered outdated. Yet somehow the quaint form of a half-dozen or so blind shots is part of its charm. Always you will be fulfilled by the challenge of the narrow fairways, the paragon of underfoot links land and lie, and the subtlety of its characteristic humps and hollows.

Visitors to a club of strict jacket-and-tie tradition are invariably captivated by the 9th hole as it steers its course back to the imposing clubhouse. It demands a high, long drive to clear the brow of the 'viewing' hill and down to a fairway 80 feet below. The line is on the spire reaching above the cluster of houses and buildings at the foot of the mountains. Then another big blow must be aimed, as if towards the town, avoiding a wickedly placed pair of bunkers en route.

In Vardon's own words, the 9th hole will exhilarate and terrify. He might have said the same about the par-three 4th hole, calling

'Exhilarating even without a club in your hand', it is said of the links laid out by Old Tom Morris at a cost 'not to exceed four guineas'.

for a 200-yard carry over the inimitable gorse and no fewer than 10 bunkers, or of the much-admired 13th hole. That's the way it is at Royal County Down.

♣ *The final round of the Irish Amateur Open Championship at Royal County Down in 1933 provided a remarkable occurrence. Eric Fiddian, the British Boys champion of 1927 and English champion of 1932, produced two holes-in-one in the course of the 36 holes match he lost by three and two to Jack McLean. Fiddian did the 7th hole of 128 yards in one in the morning and the 14th hole, 205 yards, in one in the afternoon.*

1

2

3

4

1 *Austere Royal County Down clubhouse.*
2 *The monument in recognition of Northern Ireland's second-oldest club.*
3 *'Where the Mountains of Mourne sweep down to the sea' ... the Slieve Donard Hotel, clubhouse and 9th fairway.*

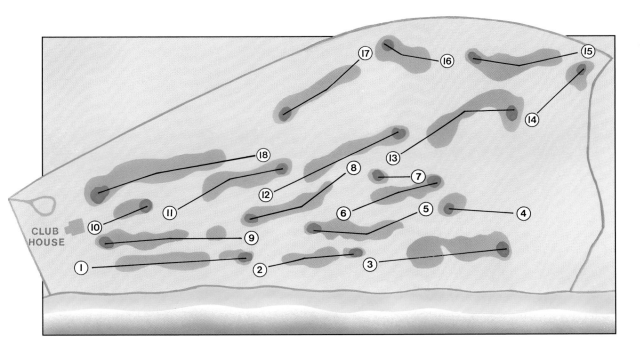

One of the club's great boasts is that, so charmed were American visitors by Royal County Down that they went back to the Cincinatti Country Club in Ohio and re-created the classic 13th hole.

4 Looking across the links to the sandy beaches of renowned Dundrum Bay.

5 A time-honoured view of Royal County Down – one of the most photographed courses in the world, and consistently one of the highest ranked.

ROYAL DUBLIN GOLF CLUB
~ YARDS: 6,889 ~ PAR: 71 ~

When Fletcher Christian and his mutinous mates consigned Captain William Bligh to the mercy of the ocean from the *Bounty* in 1789, they had little or no regard for his prospects of survival. Luckily, he did survive, otherwise there may never have been a Royal Dublin Golf Club, for the bold Captain Bligh had a hand in the creation of the land on which the links stands. He was invited to make suggestions on how to provide shipping with a safe, straight and deep approach on the River Liffey into Dublin city. The information he submitted in 1800 was helpful when the proposal for a breakwater extending from Dollymount was implemented.

The silting up that followed the building of what is known as the Bull Wall, together with nature, saw to it that the sandbank from which the island grew produced a rich crop of bent and red fescue that provides the ideal base for the greens and fairways of the Royal Dublin Club.

The club was in existence before the tract of land – now also a designated bird sanctuary – was brought into use. The Dublin

Location:
three miles east of Dublin
Type: links
Club administrator:
John A. Lamb (01-8336346)
Club professional:
Leonard Owens (01-8336477)
Best day for visitors:
weekdays except Wednesdays

Golf Club was instituted at a meeting held in 19 Grafton Street (now the city's most fashionable shopping area) in May 1885. It was granted the prefix Royal six years later.

A course had been laid by British army personnel around the Magazine Fort in Dublin's vast Phoenix Park, but the discerning pioneer members pursued a venue offering the advantages of seaside turf. For a three-year period, neighbouring Sutton proved an acceptable home, before the prime land of the North Bull Island was secured from Colonel Vernon of Clontarf in 1889.

The club sustained a major setback in 1914, when the outbreak of the First World War resulted in the links being required by the military for use as a rifle range and training centre. It was handed back four years later in a very dilapidated condition, but a £10,000 compensation award allowed the overrun course to be redesigned by E.S. Colt, a famous

1 At the elbow of Royal Dublin's infamous 'Garden' 18th hole, looking to the green and distinctive clubhouse, with the out-of-bounds garden area to the right. The hole is renowned in the story of Christy O'Connor's eagle-birdie-eagle finish to win the Carrolls Tournament.
2 Prize trophy collection.

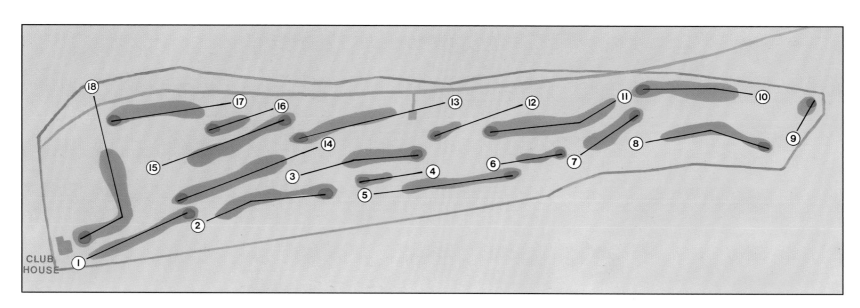

golf course architect of the time. Laid as it is on entirely flat terrain, it provides a favourable reminiscence of the Old Course at St Andrews.

The format is of the old, traditional out-and-back variety, and if the prevailing wind tends to make the front nine the easier, you will need any insurance gained for the wicked homeward journey.

Christy O'Connor Snr, who has been associated with the club since 1959, first as club professional and then as tournament pro, is loud in his praises of a place you reach by a narrow wooden bridge when he says: 'By any standards it is as good a traditional links as you will get. It is a narrower links than normal and, while I am especially taken by the variety in the four par-three holes, I know that when the course plays its true self, there is a taxing demand on long iron shots.'

The most celebrated hole is the Garden, the 463-yards par-four 18th. It is pressure all the way, with the notorious out-of-bounds 'garden' around the sharp, right-hand dog-leg. A reprieve is that the ditch marking the OB area has been declared a lateral water hazard. But three new bunkers left of the fairway, and a new one at the back right-hand corner of the green, compound the difficulty.

Christy O'Connor added to the lore of the hole by finishing his round eagle (2), birdie (3), eagle (3) (the 18th was then a par five), to win the Carrolls International Tournament in 1966.

Needless to remark for such a renowned golfing centre, Royal Dublin has housed all the leading events in Ireland. The

S.S.S.		71	73	PAR	INDEX	SCORE	
Hole	Name	Mtrs	Mtrs			A	B
1	North Bull	351	361	4	8		
2	Babington's	430	440	4	1		
3	Alps	355	363	4	9		
4	Feather Bed	157	163	3	10		
5	Valley	389	423	4	5		
6	Pot	170	180	3	17		
7	Ireland's Eye	322	338	4	12		
8	Ben Howth	435	465	5	14		
9	Davidson's	160	164	3	16		
	OUT	2769	2897	34			
10	Marne	374	378	4	3		
11	Colt's	469	479	5	11		
12	Campbell's	172	188	3	13		
13	Dardanelles	381	425	4	2		
14	Moran's	439	455	5	15		
15	Hogan's	390	397	4	6		
16	Dolly	241	245	4	18		
17	Coastguard's	341	345	4	7		
18	Garden	430	453	4	4		
	HOME	3237	3365	37			
	ADD OUT	2769	2897	34			
	TOTAL	6006	6262	71			

success of the revived Irish Open has much to do with the heady deeds of Seve Ballesteros and Bernhard Langer between 1983 and 1985. Royal Dublin has also played host to the Irish Women's Championship, the Irish

Professional Championship, the Irish Men's Native and Open Championships and, in 1962, a quite remarkable Jeyes International tournament, when David Sheahan, then a 21-year-old student and now a doctor living in Dublin, had the distinction of beating the professionals.

Royal Dublin enjoys an environment that must be unique, for it lies within the boundaries of a biosphere reserve. There are some 200 reserves throughout the world and this, the North Bull, which is the smallest, is the only one within 15 minutes' bus ride of the centre of a capital city. In the summer of 1984, an Irish scientific exped-

the links. Some people believe that it was this activity that led to his nickname, Dyke. Others claim he earned the appellation because of his ability to score one-unders, or birdies, as they are known in the modern game. To this day, the word 'dyke' is commonly used in Ireland in respect of a birdie.

4 Christy O'Connor Snr, associated with the club since 1959, plays towards the 18th. 'By any standards, this is as traditional a links as you will get,' he said.
5 A hazard for a hare in an established animal reserve.

4

1 A view from the back of the first green shows the proximity of the course to Dublin's city centre.
2 Curley's Yard, designated Museum Centre, by the 3rd and 13th holes.
3 The precision and art form of cutting new holes at Royal Dublin.

ition trapped 145 Brent geese on Bathurst Island in Arctic Canada and put coded plastic bands on their legs. Three months later, these migratory birds appeared at Royal Dublin, having covered a distance of 4,000 miles. The North Bull was officially designated a bird sanctuary as long ago as 1930.

Michael 'Dyke' Moran, after whom a nearby suburban street is named, was an interesting character who was Royal Dublin's professional from 1908 to 1914. Born and reared in a cottage in Curley's Yard, sited close by the 3rd and 13th fairways and now designated a museum centre, Moran became a caddy and was a familiar sight as he bounded over the many dykes or drains on

5

ROYAL PORTRUSH GOLF CLUB

~ DUNLUCE ~ YARDS: 7,460 ~ PAR: 72 ~
~VALLEY ~ YARDS: 6,900 ~ PAR: 70 ~

Historically significant as it truly is, it is nonetheless only part of the story to talk just in terms of Royal Portrush as the only golf club in Ireland to have hosted the British Open Championship. The proud appellation was earned in July 1951, when the only Open ever staged outside Britain was won by the flamboyant Max Faulkner with 285, four under par.

If that is the high point in the history of the club, founded in 1888 and granted the Royal prefix seven years later, when the Prince of Wales (later King Edward VII) was invited to become patron, Royal Portrush

Location:
one mile from Portrush town

Type: links

Club administrator:
Ms Wilma Erskine (01265-822311)

Club professional:
Dai Stevenson (0265-823335)

Best day for visitors:
avoid Wednesdays, Fridays (p.m.), Saturdays

has always been in the shop window as a championship venue.

The British Amateur Championship returns in 1993, thus retaining a trend dating back to 1895, when the club's first professional, Sandy Herd, beat the celebrity Harry Vardon in the first professional event ever staged in Ireland.

Another landmark was that the Ladies' Championship of 1898 marked the first occasion on which that particular event was played outside Britain. The first Irish Native Professional Championship was played in 1907, and many times, especially in the important formative years of organised golf in Ireland, Royal Portrush was the bulwark of the National Men's and Ladies' Championships.

Significantly, the area, which of course is also one of the best-known seaside holiday resorts in Ireland, bred many a famous player. It was here that Fred Daly, Ireland's only British Open champion (Hoylake, 1947) learned to play, and the golf-oriented town also weaned other renowned characters such as twice British champion Rhona Adair, the Walker Cup player and Irish international G.N.C. Martin, as well as the influential Beck, Bolton and Hezlet families. That is a measure of Portrush's influence on golf.

1 *Harry Colt's 6th green, named in recognition of the British amateur's architectural genius.*

2 *War Hollow 4th fairway on the adjoining valley course.*
3 *Local tourist attraction: the Giant's Causeway.*

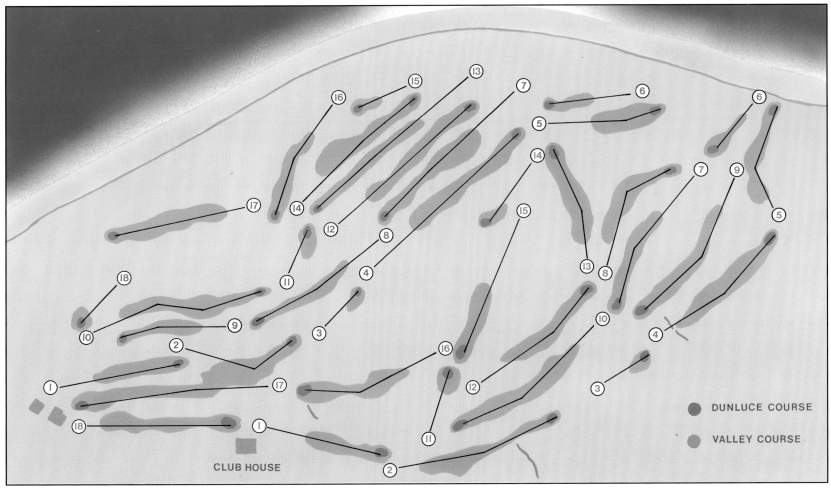

DUNLUCE COURSE

VALLEY COURSE

CLUB HOUSE

1 The medal won by Fred Daly in the British Open, Hoylake, 1947, and presented to the club by Ireland's only Open champion.
2 Beautiful 5th green location, endangered by Atlantic coastal erosion!

3 Purgatory, offering no reprieve after the adventure of Calamity (6), the club's most notorious hole.
4 The rugged 13th green setting.

5 Halfway tavern offering a 'wee dram'!
7 Tumbling to Dunluce and Valley courses, with the resort town in background.

| Hole | Name | YARDS | | | Par | Stroke Index |
		Champ. Blue	Medal White	Society Green		
1	Hughies	389	381	371	4	7
2	Giant's Grave	497	493	477	5	11
3	Islay	159	150	140	3	17
4	Fred Daly's	455	454	442	4	3
5	White Rocks	384	380	369	4	9
6	Harry Colt's	193	187	177	3	15
7	Tavern	432	420	415	4	1
8	Himalayas	376	365	358	4	13
9	Warren	478	476	456	5	5
		3363	3306	3205	36	
10	Dhu Varren	480	477	461	5	10
11	Feather Bed	166	166	162	3	18
12	Causeway	395	389	367	4	2
13	Skerries	371	366	358	4	6
14	Calamity	213	205	195	3	16
15	Purgatory	366	361	357	4	12
16	Babington	432	415	404	4	4
17	Glenarm	517	508	496	5	14
18	Greenaway	469	457	456	4	8
	In	3409	3344	3256	36	
	Out	3363	3306	3205	36	
	Total	6772	6650	6461	72	
	S.S.S.	73	73	72	H'cap	
					Net	

4

Recognised as chief rival to Lahinch for the honour of being known as the 'St Andrews of Ireland', Royal Portrush, which is sited a mere drive and pitch from the holiday town, is a well-equipped facility of three courses: the No. 1, or Dunluce, on the higher and more open ground; the less challenging though greatly appealing Valley Course in the historic War Hollow, where local lore has it that the Chief of Dunluce fought the King of Norway many centuries ago; and then the nine-hole pitch and putt course called, because of the island to be viewed in an eastward direction, the Skerries.

The unique Royal Portrush complex, just an hour's drive north from Belfast, and within easy reach of more great links courses at Castlerock, Portstewart and Ballycastle, is the original work of Harry Colt. The noted British amateur's architectural portfolio also included Wentworth, Rye, Sunningdale New and the Eden course at St Andrews (also some alterations at Royal Dublin), and if it is held that the man's admiration for the

5

6

CALAMITY

No. 14
YARDS
213
PAR 3
S.I. 16

7

Old Course at St Andrews influenced his design concept, then all the better!

At Portrush, layout perception was enhanced by location, a factor that convinced the club's early pioneers to move closer to the sea. Nature bestowed such gifts that both courses are laid out in a marvellous span of country forming a magnificent stretch of golden sand on two sides, and the Antrim Coast Road leading out to the famous Giant's Causeway on the other.

Everyone is enraptured by the scenery, which takes account of the hills of Donegal to the west and, to the north, looking towards Scotland, the hazy outline of Islay and the Hebrides. Don't be carried away by it all; Royal Portrush demands absolute concentration as straight driving is a must (ten

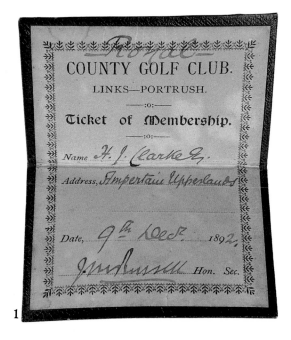

1

holes bend left or right), and heavy rough is plentiful at one of the world's greatest golfing venues.

Unfortunately, a price that has to be paid for the setting is the recurring problem of coastal erosion. When the raging seas of one particular winter took their savage revenge on the exposed point encompassing the

1 *An early membership card.*
2 *The influence of the St Andrews*
Old Course shows in the design of the greens.
3 *Evidence that ladies were*
influential in the club's development.
4 *Fred Daly's Hole, in memory of the*
legendary locally born golfer.
5 *No. 13 ... the Skerries, 371, par four.*
6 *Old golf bag ID tags.*

2

classic par-four fifth, and the one-shot gem of a sixth hole, Joe Carr, who had won, in 1960, the last of his three British Amateur Championships on the links, was moved to plead, 'These links are one of the great heritages of golf and must be protected for present and future generations of golfers.'

The 1993 Captain of the Royal and Ancient Golf Club of St Andrews spoke for us all!

☘ *No hole in golf is more aptly named than Calamity Corner, adventurous site of the par three 14th hole (championship tee 215 yards, medal tee 205 yards). The most severe 'one-shotter' in Ireland – in golf? – is perched on a cliff edge, and if you fail to negotiate the bold carry and drop into the chasm on the right, you are dead! For the faint-hearted there is the option to sacrifice the thrill of*

3

4

5

6

going for broke with a bale-out shot into Bobby Locke's Hollow to the left entrance of the green. Either way, be forewarned: the following hole is named Purgatory!

☘ *A long-preserved and cherished tradition is the hoisting of the flag over the halfway tavern by the 10th tee, indicating that a 'wee dram' is available as sustenance for the continuing battle.*

1

2

3

TRALEE GOLF CLUB
~ YARDS: 6,961 ~ PAR: 71 ~

When Arnold Palmer was commissioned to design his first golf course in Europe, he promised the expectant members of Tralee that he would build them a masterpiece. He kept his word.

Palmer won the tender from a host of the world's leading golf course designers. All of them shared the common view that the site at Barrow was a rare one, bestowed by nature itself.

Palmer extracted full dividends from the stunningly beautiful landscape overlooking Banna Strand, a location used in the making of David Lean's blockbuster film *Ryan's Daughter*, when the ambitious Tralee club vacated its 'downtown' nine-hole course at Mount Hawk, in existence since 1907.

While Palmer himself was always convinced that the land was 'so ideally suited for the building of a golf course', he also found a disciple in one Peter Dobereiner, the noted British golf writer now pursuing a design career.

Dobereiner became so enthralled at what he discovered that he wrote: 'Robert Louis Stevenson got it wrong when he described the Monterey Peninsula as the finest conjunction of land and sea this earth has to offer. As a spectacle, Tralee is in a different class!'

The lore of Tralee is captured in fanciful names assigned to some holes: Cú Chullain's Table, the narrow par-four 4th , where the great warrior Cú Chullain is said to have dined on his visits to Barrow with the Fianna; Brandon, the quietly dog-legging 5th hole

Location: Barrow

Type: links

Hon. Secretary:
Donal O'Connell (066-36379)

No professional

Best day for visitors:
welcome, but limited on
Wednesdays and weekends

looking towards Mt Brendan and named after St Brendan the navigator, whose famous voyage is depicted in the club badge; the 7th hole, called the Randy in deference to a meeting place of smugglers; Palmer's

Peak, the long, par-five 11th, offering panoramic views of the Dingle Peninsula; and the emotive Shipwreck, the dramatic par-three, steeply downhill 16th of around 190 yards, where lack of care could shipwreck

1 *Dizzy par-three Brock's Hollow, looking back over the chasm to the tee.*
2 *Overlooking Banna Strand, the location for the film* Ryan's Daughter.
3 *The perilous, rocky Atlantic shoreline, to be carried with the tee shot to the fabulous 3rd hole.*
4 *Ominous clouds gather as players pass on the adjoining fairways.*

your hopes among the rusted ruins of many wrecks.

At Palmer's favourite part of the course you will find the Castle backing onto the spectacular par-three 3rd hole. It conjures up the frightening aspect of a Pebble Beach and Cypress Point, where the mid iron tee shot has to be hit by the edge of the cliff and against the distracting background music of pounding Atlantic waves.

By rich irony, the clifftop setting presented its own problems. In the early stages of development the howling winds and sea spray from the Atlantic defied all attempts to grow grass. Successive winter gales were especially destructive, but the patience of the members, and trial and error by the management, productively combined

1

2

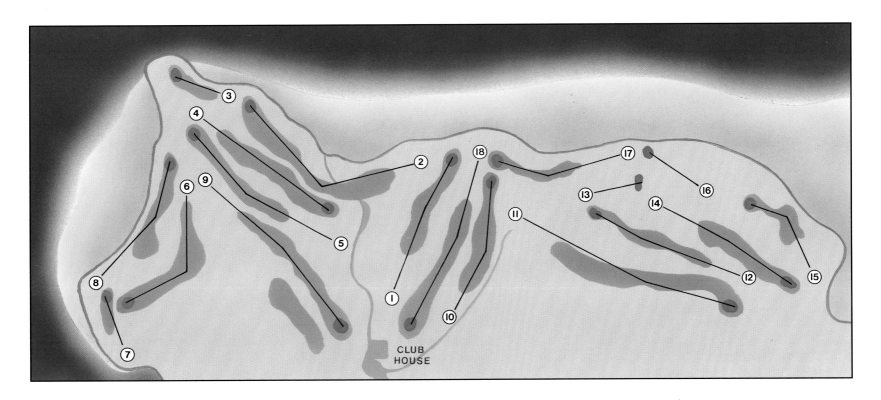

to produce a course of a quality befitting its rare location – and the wisdom of Arnold Palmer.

🍀 *Tralee is the principal town of County Kerry, and each year the thriving industrial and trading centre stages the glamorous International Rose of Tralee Festival. Many thousands come to play golf and to see for themselves the …*

> *Pale moon rising, above the green mountain,*
> *The sun declining beneath the blue sea,*
> *That made me love Mary,*
> *The Rose of Tralee.*

🍀 *The old castle ruin, as depicted in Tralee's coat of arms, is a Tudor gun-turret based on a design by Henry VIII, at a part of the course near Barrow Point, where ancient law decrees that balls lost in the ocean belong to one Geoffrey de Clahuill, who was granted, according to equally ancient folklore, the wrecks of the sea by King John.*

3

1 *Beautiful view from the 5th hole of the old Tudor gun-turret, Barrow Harbour and Mount Brandon.*
2 *Tralee's showpiece view to the 3rd green, near the preserved Castle based on a design by Henry VIII.*

3 *Appropriately-named Shipwreck, the dramatic par-three 16th of 181 yards, set on a clifftop at a point where local lore holds that the wrecks of many ships lie buried!*
4 *The elevated teeing site down to the 16th green.*

4

HOLE	NAME	BLUE METRES	WHITE METRES	PAR	Stroke Index
1	Mucklough	367	355	4	12
2	The Cuilin	537	516	5	2
3	The Castle	175	140	3	14
4	Cuchullain's Table	392	366	4	8
5	Brandon	389	374	4	4
6	Chough's Corner	380	374	4	10
7	The Randy	142	135	3	18
8	The Creek	356	339	4	6
9	Hare's Lane	451	443	5	16
OUT		3189	3042	36	
10	The Warren	390	370	4	9
11	Palmer's Peak	531	514	5	7
12	Bracken	408	400	4	1
13	Brock's Hollow	146	139	3	15
14	Crosty	370	361	4	5
15	Poulgorm	279	267	4	17
16	Shipwreck	181	152	3	11
17	Ryan's Daughter	321	304	4	13
18	The Goat's Hole	424	403	4	3
IN		3050	2910	35	
OUT		3189	3042	36	
TOT.		6239	5952		
NETT RESULT		HANDICAP			
			NETT		

TRAMORE GOLF CLUB
~ YARDS: 6,597 ~ PAR: 72 ~

That extracts from a booklet called *Tramore – The Riviera of Ireland* and published over 50 years ago have stood the test of time is itself telling testimony to the status and standard of Tramore Golf Club.

Whatever the claim relating to the Riviera, Tramore, the archetypical seaside holiday resort on the south-east coast, nine miles from Waterford city, of cut glass crystal fame, certainly boasts a parkland golfing amenity surpassing most others of its type.

The citation reads: 'The view from the clubhouse is magnificent, embracing as it does practically the whole course with the lofty Comeragh Mountains in the distant background. A sunset view from this vantage point is something to be treasured in one's memory forever. On this site, which is gently undulating, intercepted by two streams, Capt. H.C. Tippet of Walton Heath has laid out as magnificent an 18-hole links as ever pleased the eye.' There are few golfers who would disagree.

The late and renowned Henry Cotton shared the general opinion of Tramore's greatness. 'The 17th hole is one of the best in these Islands,' he announced, in salute to a popularly perceived example of one of the club's many highlights.

1 *The club's Roll of Honour, dating back to 1894.*
2 *An example of the contention that Tramore is as good a course 'as ever pleased the eye'.*

Location: half a mile from Tramore, on Dungarvan coast road

Type: parkland

Club administrator:
Jim Cox (051-386170)

Club professional:
Derry Kiely (051-86170)

Best day for visitors:
avoid weekends

No.	Blue	White	Yellow	Par	Index	A	B
		METRES					
1	367	367	354	4	6		
2	449	449	424	5	11		
3	157	157	146	3	15		
4	329	329	313	4	3		
5	297	297	295	4	12		
6	157	157	137	3	17		
7	363	363	354	4	8		
8	369	369	351	4	2		
9	500	500	468	5	9		
out	2988	2988	2842	36			
10	172	172	152	3	16		
11	363	332	321	4	4		
12	317	317	309	4	10		
13	368	331	321	4	7		
14	405	368	345	4	1		
15	114	114	109	3	18		
16	483	483	450	5	13		
17	341	319	297	4	5		
18	447	447	419	5	14		
in	3010	2883	2723	36			
S.S.S.	71	70	69				

The hole is a dog-leg set between lines of mature trees, close by which is sited the club's fascinating pheasant farm, where you will discover the green coyly placed between a giant bunker to the apron side, ready to snare the indecisive, and then clinging vegetation at the rear, poised to punish the overzealous!

Placement, rather than aggressive length, is seen to be the determining factor at Tramore. Yet it is only in recent times that local amateur hot-shot Eddie Power was the first to complete a round as low as 65 shots.

The need for the invaluable trait of accuracy is hardly surprising, since hitting the green at the 172 yards short third hole

is a hard-learned case of 'be on the green, or else!'

The same dictum applies at the exceptionally tight par four 11th hole, where a line of trees, some bunkers and streams are optional diversions.

2

Indulging in the panoramic view of colourfully attractive forests, streams and heather from the clubhouse, it is difficult to imagine that not a single tree was in existence when the club moved to this prime site, a casual stroll out of town, back in 1939.

It is remarkable how successful was the mammoth task undertaken by determined members to transform what was largely marshland into the gem you may appreciate today.

1 Action in the formative years of the club before the original course was washed away.
2 The attractive entrance to the 4th green amid the plentiful gorse.

1

2

3

4

Tramore's distinctive club badge depicts the Sea Horse, *an ill-fated three-deck, three-masted fighting vessel commanded by Nelson in 1799. Following the Battle of Waterloo it was wrecked in Tramore Bay around 1816, when many lives were lost. The same heavy seas were responsible 100 years later for the obliteration of the club's first course, situated in the sandhills by the shoreline.*

3 The 12th hole, where trees, bunkers and streams are enduring hazards.
4 At one time treeless marshland, now a blazing oasis!
5 Clubhouse crystal, world-renowned product from nearby Waterford.
6 Tramore's imposing Round Robin Trophy.

5

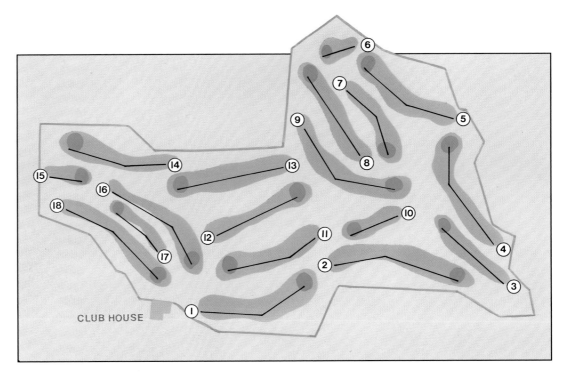

CLUB HOUSE

TULLAMORE GOLF CLUB
~ YARDS: 6,314 ~ PAR: 72 ~

It was a happy case of sixth time being lucky for Tullamore when they discovered their present home in 1926. In terms of parkland locations, it has few peers.

Even if Tullamore's status falls into the less daunting category of challenges, it is nevertheless widely appreciated that when James Braid reconstructed the layout in 1938 he produced one of his better works.

The King's course at Gleneagles, and the British Open rota courses at Turnberry and Royal Troon, as well as Carnoustie, each prospered by the hand of the five-times Open champion. So it is that the humble Scot, of whom it was said that he hit the ball with 'a divine fury', also left a lasting legacy at Tullamore, where to state that his vision from a bygone era has stood the test of time is to grasp the subtle challenge.

There is an appealing sense of the well preserved amid the towering oak, because complementing the quaint course is the ambience of a low-level, cosy clubhouse with an attractive picture bay window design.

The combination paints a picture of why the Tullamore club is a focal point in an area of the unassuming midlands of Ireland, well known for its bog, its ancient monastic settlements and its castles.

Charleville is said to be the finest and most spectacular 19th-century Gothic

1-2 Towering oak, an enduring feature of the quaint Tullamore course, laid out by James Braid.

Location: three miles south-west of Tullamore town

Type: parkland

Hon. Secretary:
Pat Burns (0506-21439)

Club professional:
Donagh McArdle (0506-51757)

Best day for visitors:
avoid Tuesdays

revival building in Ireland. To the west is the famous early Celtic monastery where the last High King of Ireland, Rory O'Connor, was buried in 1198. North of Tullamore is the site of the famous Monastery of Durrow, founded by St Columcille.

Tullamore is also noted as having originally distilled the elixirs Tullamore Dew and Irish Mist.

It is to Braid's eternal credit that he maximised the value of the many tree species. His perception accounts for the lure of the dog-leg, index-one, 460-yards 5th hole; for

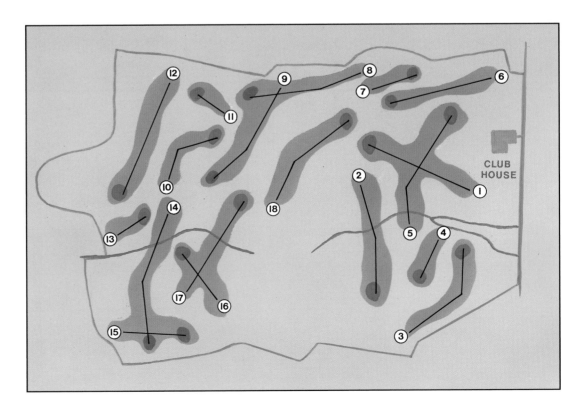

the clever placement of the 160-yards par-three 7th hole, where the green is tucked into a cluster of trees and, similarly, for the attractive manner in which the fairway to the 9th green lies through an enchanting leafy avenue.

Also contributing to the appealing golf course is the lazy stream which meanders with potential destruction for the unwary across your path at the 2nd, 5th, 14th and 17th holes.

The best professional exponents were respectfully mindful of the pitfalls when they played the Native Irish Championship here in 1967 and returned for the Dunlop Tournament in 1970. Coincidentally, each title was won by the same player: the Ryder

Cup man Hugh Boyle. His stock in trade was a telling facility to keep the ball down the straight and narrow.

The demands at Tullamore are clearly illustrated in the finishing three holes. Anyone needing to score level par, i.e. 3-4-5, will surely test the nerves with a long drive away from the right-hand OB boundary fence at the uphill par-five 18th. At 510 yards, it is the longest hole on the course.

1 *The Brisco Perpetual Cup for keen club competition.*
2 *How Braid maximised the value of rare tree species.*
3 *Enchanting leafy avenues on the Tullamore course.*

Holes	Yards	Metres	Par	Strokes Index
1	312	286	4	17
2	515	471	5	5
3	360	329	4	7
4	170	156	3	13
5	460	420	4	1
6	351	321	4	9
7	160	146	3	15
8	407	372	4	3
9	493	450	5	11
	3228	2951	36	
10	433	396	4	2
11	220	201	3	8
12	478	437	5	14
13	127	116	3	18
14	376	343	4	6
15	308	282	4	16
16	195	178	3	12
17	382	349	4	4
18	510	466	5	10
	3029	2768	35	
	3228	2951	36	
	6257	5719	71	

🍀 *Tullamore's John Kelly, holds the distinction of being the longest-serving professional at one club. He has been in residence since 1950.*

🍀 *Katherine 'Kitty' MacCann is Tullamore's most distinguished member. Winner of the British Amateur Open Championship in 1951, a cruel stroke of fate prevented her from playing for Britain and Ireland in the historic Curtis Cup match against the United States at Muirfield in 1952. Chosen for the final day's singles matches, she was taken ill and missed the chance of helping B and I to their first ever victory over the Americans.*

4 Proud residential record by club professional John Kelly, attached since 1950: an Irish record.
5 The club's most famous player, Mrs P.G. 'Kitty' McCann, twice Irish Champion and British Open winner.

6 Nice shot, well rewarded on greens of lasting repute.
7 Landmark opening of new pavilion at Brookfield, 1926.

5

6

7

WATERVILLE GOLF CLUB
~ YARDS: 7,184 ~ PAR: 72 ~

The fact that access to Waterville Golf Club is via the world-renowned Ring of Kerry tourist route tells its own story.

Given that the principal elements in the beauty of County Kerry are water – sea and lake – and mountains, the tiny village situated in the most south-western peninsula of Ireland stands apart.

Long before Irish-American John A. Mulcahy became captivated in the mid-1970s by the picturesque oasis, bordered on one side by the Kerry Mountains and on the other by Ballinskelligs Bay, and was inspired to transform a largely decaying nine-hole course into a famous golf resort (the course is now owned by a New York consortium), the seaside village was established through reputation as a restful, get-away-from-it-all fishing location.

The late movie actor Charlie Chaplin for many years brought his family on holiday here, to his beloved retreat at the local Butler Arms Hotel.

Location: one mile from the village					
Type: links					
Club administrator: Noel J. Cronin (066-74102)					
Club professional: Liam Higgins (066-74237)					
Best day for visitors: any day					

Names	No.	Blue	Par	White	Index
Last Easy	1	430	4	395	11
Christy's Choice	2	469	4	425	1
Innyside	3	417	4	362	3
The Dunes	4	179	3	160	15
Tipperary	5	595	5	525	9
Heaven's Highway	6	371	4	343	13
The Island	7	178	3	155	17
Ponderous	8	435	4	410	5
Prodigal	9	445	4	405	7
		3519	35	3180	
Bottleneck	10	475	4	450	2
Tranquility	11	496	5	477	10
The Mass Hole	12	200	3	154	18
The Twin	13	518	5	480	14
The Judge	14	456	4	410	4
The Vale	15	392	4	365	6
Liam's Ace	16	350	4	330	12
Mulcahy's Peak	17	196	3	153	16
O'Grady's Beach	18	582	5	550	8
Competition		3665	37	3369	
		7184	72	6549	
S.S.		74			

Fishing continues to be one of the attractions, though golfers account for the larger numbers of tourists, which is no wonder when you take account of the largely uncrowded nature of a course dubbed 'the beautiful monster – one of the golfing wonders of the world' by Sam Snead, famed US Masters and British Open winner.

Another notability, Raymond Floyd, the former Ryder Cup captain and player, enthused, 'Waterville is one of the most beautiful places I have ever seen, with the finest links holes I have ever played.' His contemporary Tom Watson was moved to declare: 'Apart from anything else, Waterville possesses the best par three holes I have ever encountered on the same golf course.'

That sentiment by the US Ryder Cup team captain encapsulates a particularly unforgettable Waterville feature: the par-three 17th hole of 196 yards. Named Mulcahy's Peak in honour of the man who founded the present club, it is one of the most

1 Ancient implements can be traced to the 1800s, when foreigners introduced golf while laying trans-Atlantic cable.
2 A fascinating feature hole, the 17th, named after John A. Mulcahy, who loved the view from the high-rise teeing area.
3 Christy's Choice – a favourite of the Ryder Cup legend.
4 Panoramic view from the 17th tee.

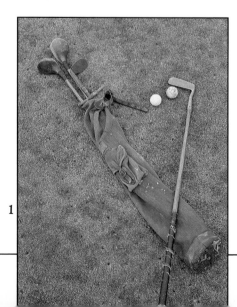

1

MULCAHY'S PEAK

THIS HOLE IS NAMED AFTER THE DEVELOPER OF THIS LINKS, IRISH-AMERICAN, JOHN A. MULCAHY, WHO USED TO STAND ON THE HIGH POINT ABOVE AND SCAN THE MAJESTIC PANORAMA, WHILE LAYING OUT THE COURSE IN HIS MIND'S EYE. WHEN THE LINKS WAS DESIGNED, HE INSISTED THAT A TEE BE PLACED HERE, SO THAT ALL WHO PLAY WATERVILLE WOULD DEPART WITH A REMEMBRANCE OF THIS UNIQUE SETTING.

2

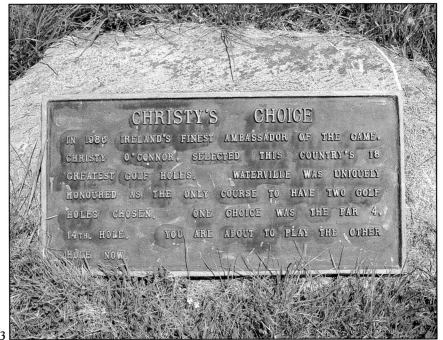

CHRISTY'S CHOICE

IN 1986 IRELAND'S FINEST AMBASSADOR OF THE GAME, CHRISTY O'CONNOR, SELECTED THIS COUNTRY'S 18 GREATEST GOLF HOLES. WATERVILLE WAS UNIQUELY HONOURED AS THE ONLY COURSE TO HAVE TWO GOLF HOLES CHOSEN. ONE CHOICE WAS THE PAR 4, 14TH HOLE. YOU ARE ABOUT TO PLAY THE OTHER HOLE NOW.

3

4

1 *The green at the celebrated Mass Hole, the par-three 12th.*
2 *Christy's Choice – and an example of what 'Himself' means.*
3 *Rolling fairway onto the 15th green.*

4 *Hole 2 – Christy's Choice – Index 1!*
5 *Teeing ground to the 12th, played across a deep gorge, where locals conducted clandestine religious meetings in Penal Days.*

1

2

3

4

difficult holes you will ever play.

The tee stands a dizzy 250 feet above sea level. If you can keep your nerve, you can indulge in the panoramic beauty of contrasting sea and mountainside. More engaging will be how to negotiate your tee shot of almost 200 yards over uncharted dunes described as 'an emerald oasis amidst a jungle of nature's own terrain.'

To finish the 17th hole with the same ball is one objective: to come off the green with a par is reward indeed!

Always bear in mind at Waterville that the Atlantic winds are unrelenting. They can affect every shot, especially over the tough finishing stretch from the 16th, hard by the exposure of Ballinskelligs Bay. Earlier on, it is the River Inny against which you must be on guard, through the attractive stretch of holes two, three and four.

When asked to nominate his favourite

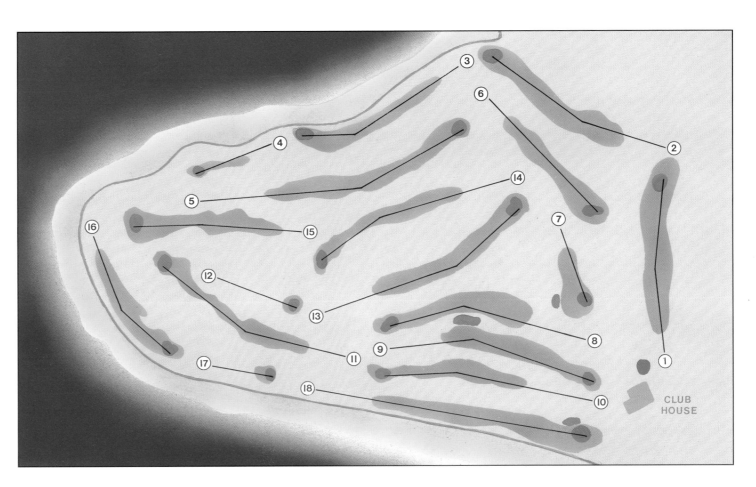

18 holes in Ireland, the legendary Christy O'Connor Snr picked two from among Waterville's gems. 'Christy's Choice' is the name given in his honour to the left-to-right tilting, 469-yards par-four second. Christy also nominated the 456-yards par-four 14th, sternly named the Judge. Playing it, you will know why.

They are the essence of the Waterville experience.

🍀 *Golf at Waterville can be traced back to the mid-1800s, not, peculiarly, in view of tradition in Ireland, due to the influence of British Army regiments, but to the foreigners who came to lay the trans-Atlantic cable and who were stationed on Valentia Island, just off the coast.*

🍀 *Among the many features of the Waterville course is the par-three 12th hole, played across a deep gorge. It is named the Mass Hole, a throwback to the Penal Times in Ireland, when the local inhabitants celebrated their religion in the concealed hollow for fear of persecution.*

WESTPORT GOLF CLUB

~ *YARDS: 6,959 ~ PAR: 73 ~*

A whimsical old story from times long past tells that when St Patrick wanted to rid Ireland of all its snakes, he rang a bell on a precipice by the side of Croagh Patrick and, lemming-like, they threw themselves over the mountainside. The tale is told of a pilgrim spot that attracts many thousands of visitors each year, the more devout of whom climb the 2,500-foot mountain bare footed.

On the Westport golf course spread serenely below, despairing golfers often ponder if they have their priorities right as

Location: two miles from Westport town

Type: parkland

Club administrator:
Pat Smyth (098-28262)

Club professional:
Alex Mealia (098-27481)

Best day for visitors:
welcome all week

they seek Divine inspiration in the shadow of the Holy Mountain.

Although golf has been played since 1927 in the bustling Co. Mayo seaside tourist resort, hard by Clew Bay and looking out towards the striking silhouette of Clare Island, it was only in 1973 that the club moved the one mile to its present location.

Partly perched on a clifftop overlooking the island-strewn bay of fishing renown, Westport is essentially a parkland course. Its layout is by the distinguished hand of Fred Hawtree Jnr, who has also, among his wide architectural briefs, been involved with update work at Royal Birkdale and Royal Liverpool. To give this noted British designer his due, he has done a fine job at Westport.

The unsuspecting should be warned not to be lulled into a false sense of security by the comparatively easy-playing nature of the opening half dozen holes. For instance, the 9th hole, hitting out of a cluster of trees and aiming 176 yards up to a tilted and jealously bunkered green, by the bank of the commanding clubhouse, represents as mean a finish to a nine-hole stretch as you will be

1 *The jealously-guarded 9th green beside the glass-fronted clubhouse.*
2 *The view over the 16th green towards towering Croagh Patrick.*
3 *Perhaps the most intimidating tee shot in Irish golf: the drive over Clew Bay, as the starting point to the memorable 580-yard 15th hole.*

Hole No.	LENGTH (Yards)		Par	Index
	C'Ship Tees	Medal Tees		
1	348	335	4	16
2	343	330	4	10
3	162	149	3	18
4	501	488	5	14
5	356	343	4	12
6	453	445	4	4
7	524	511	5	8
8	468	455	4	2
9	202	196	3	6
OUT	3357	3252	36	
10	517	498	5	11
11	433	420	4	1
12	220	208	3	7
13	455	442	4	3
14	189	180	3	9
15	580	515	5	5
16	363	350	4	15
17	316	303	4	17
18	520	499	5	13
IN	3593	3415	37	
OUT	3357	3252	36	
Gross	6950	6667	73	

1 No 'animal' trespassers!
2 Man at work in Heavenly retreat.
3 Sea mist gathers over Clew Bay and
the surrounding mountain tops.
4 Outline of the climb to the green at
the par-five 15th.

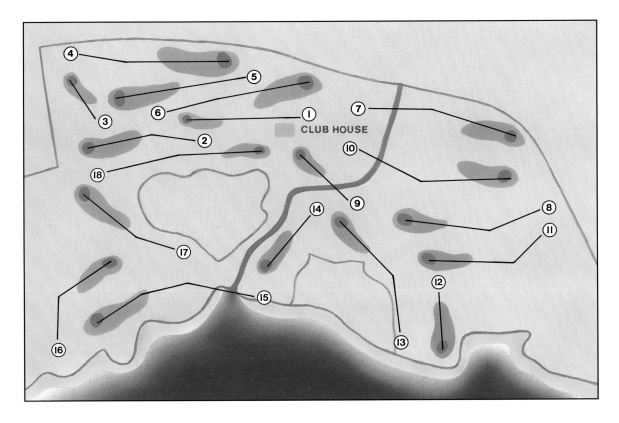

iably seems to play even longer than its prescribed 208 yards, requires a full-blooded tee shot (or would driver be more accurately descriptive?), aimed to sea, while the 14th, at around 160 yards, is a more dainty affair, even though the high green backs onto the Atlantic seashore.

It is at this critical juncture that Westport begins to show its teeth. The formidable 15th sets the tone!

Because of its location close to mountains and the sea, Westport is rich in bird and animal life. The lands of the club are preserved.

The longest hole on the card, the 560-yards par-five 15th, is also Westport's much-acclaimed highlight. More than its length, it is the perilous positioning of the tee and then the switch-back contour of the right-to-left, lengthy fairway that combines to give it its fearsome reputation.

5 Stone-wall boundary line, synonymous with the West of Ireland, and in the background a place of pilgrimage associated with St Patrick.
6 The welcoming, timber-beamed ambience of Westport's popular 19th hole.

asked to encounter anywhere.

By coincidence, two more par threes highlight other endearing features of a course that has already hosted two memorable Irish amateur native champion-ships and whose popularity has been increased by the building of the nearby Knock International Airport.

The downhill 12th hole, which invar-

The drive must be smacked off a raised tee to carry over the rocky shores of the ocean. It is fully 200 yards to the safety of dry land. Even then there is no let up, as it will take another thundering wood (and probably more) to make much headway towards the green. All the while, you must steer a path away from the ever-present and intimidating sight of the Atlantic, just beyond the out-of-bounds fencing.

WOODBROOK GOLF CLUB
~ YARDS: 6,595 ~ PAR: 72 ~

The history of tournament golf in Ireland is enriched all the more because of the acknowledged part that Woodbrook has played in inspiring so many magic and imperishable moments.

It also explains why there is a nostalgic air of occasion and tradition reaching out to the visitor. The stirring evidence is to hand, whether in the warmth of the snug, part Tudor-styled clubhouse, or around the marvellous collection of holes on a course set so scenically on a clifftop between the broad sweep of the Irish Sea into Dublin Bay and the Sugar Loaf landmark in the Wicklow Mountains.

The heavens still echo to the wild cheers that marked the staging of so many memorable tournaments here. From the late 1950s there was the Irish Hospitals Sweeps tournament, which gave way to the halcyon days of the Carrolls International tournaments in the 1960s and 1970s, and on to its climax in 1975, when the Irish Open was revived after 22 years.

In every way, it can be truthfully said that the Co. Wicklow club, a neighbour to the popular Bray seaside tourist resort, has played a significant part in the phenomenal growth of interest in golf in Ireland. Synonymous with the ideal venue for big-time golf are the much-chronicled exploits of Christy O'Connor Snr.

An older generation still treasures a Monday morning in 1960, when so many people found reason not to go to work and were witnesses to the course record 63

Location: 11 miles south-east of Dublin city

Type: parkland

Club administrator:
Jim Melody (01-2824799)

Club professional:
Billy Kinsella (01-2824799)

Best day for visitors:
avoid Tuesdays and public holidays

scored by 'Himself' when beating Ken Bousfield in a play-off to the Hospitals Sweeps tournament. Sunday lunch was abandoned by the mums and dads of Dublin on another play-off occasion, when all the family were taken out to cheer Christy as he beat the Argentine Roberto de Vicenzo for the Carrolls title in 1964. The Royal Dublin maestro won again in 1967 and 1972 and, of course, it was the turn of another of the O'Connor clan, Christy Jnr, to thrill the partisan crowds when he beat a star international field – including freshly crowned British Open champion Tom Watson – for the Irish Open title in the year of its revival.

The international appeal of these great annual occasions was highlighted, too, by the success of the Australian Kel Nagle. His 24 under par score of 260 in 1960 stood as the record low 72-holes total on the European Tour for almost 30 years. A Woodbrook achievement from those heady times which still endures is the effort by amateur Tom Craddock in marking down five twos (four birdies and an eagle) on his card during the 1967 Carrolls tournament.

1 *The only reminder of cricketing days at Woodbrook is the bell, which used to toll for the start and close of play.*
2 *Cliff-top boundary line looking north over the Irish Sea to Killiney Head. The coastline is being eroded by the sea, endangering Woodbrook's lovely location.*

Hole	Metres	Par	Index
1	455	5	13
2	165	3	5
3	345	4	7
4	354	4	3
5	446	5	15
6	295	4	11
7	393	4	1
8	326	4	9
9	116	3	17
OUT	2895	36	
10	334	4	6
11	165	3	12
12	465	5	8
13	150	3	14
14	449	5	10
15	385	4	2
16	442	5	16
17	123	3	18
18	337	4	4
IN	2850	36	
TOTAL	5745	72	

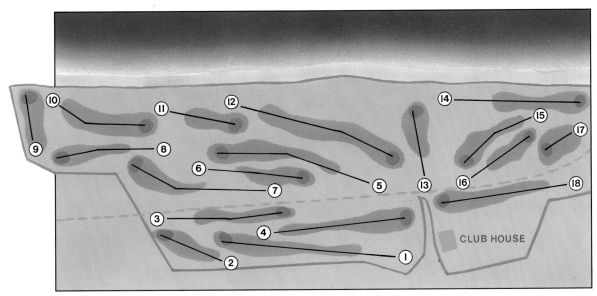

Much of the allure of Woodbrook to anyone with a feeling for history is that when the club was formally affiliated to the Golfing Union of Ireland in 1926 it was following a fascinating cricket tradition.

The club was owned by a remarkable man: Sir Stanley Cochrane of the mineral water company. He lived in that lovely house by the right of the driveway to the clubhouse. A cricket buff, Cochrane's great wealth allowed him to indulge his passion with such relish that he formed a club known as Woodbrook Club and Ground.

It cannot be ascertained whether or not the immortal W.G. Grace appeared in one of the many matches played. Among those who did, however, were such household names as Jack Hobbs, Sydney Barnes and Frank Wooley of Kent; Hirst and Rhodes of Yorkshire; Warren Bardsley and Ernie Cotter of Australia, and the South Africans Aubrey Faulkner and David Nourse.

The cricketing influence explains why there is a railway siding on which golfers now walk en route from the fourth green across the tracks to the fifth tee. Cochrane persuaded the rail authorities to provide the facility so that enthusiasts could come to watch the cricket!

1

2

3

4

Today the railway line can add a frightening dimension to a round of golf. Its presence is too close for comfort when you are playing half a dozen of the holes. Visitors find it hard to credit that the railway line once ran along the clifftop, and the story about why it had to be moved inland highlights the on-going worry for the members concerning destruction by coastal erosion.

It is a pretty precarious walk along the cliffs (heed the Danger signposts!) when playing the 9th, 10th, 11th, 12th and 14th. Ground is being washed away to such an alarming degree that a sentence of death hangs over the lovely little 9th hole, where the green totters uncomfortably close to the sea, in which many an over-clubbed shot has found a watery grave.

The 10th hole, the par-three 11th and the fairway of the dog-leg, par-five 12th all run parallel to the cliff. It's an invigorating stretch of the course as the sea breezes add to the challenge, although your heart goes out to a club partly endangered by its own lovely location.

1 Woodbrook's snug, Tudor-style clubhouse and decorative surrounds.
2 The par-three 9th green overhanging the clifftop!
3 Danger – trains passing!
4 Danger – cliffs eroding!
5 The 11th green, facing towards Killiney and Dalkey Island.
6 Heading southeast towards picturesque Bray Head, seen from the area of the 13th green and 14th tee.

IRISH GOLF COURSES

Main picture: *The new Malahide Golf Club.*
Top: *Links golf at Ceann Sibéal.*
Above: *Clifftop Howth Golf Club.*

IRISH GOLF COURSES

Abbeyfeale
Dromtrasna Collins, Abbeyfeale, Co. Limerick. Tel: 068-32033
Undemanding and hospitable 18-hole parkland club.

Abbeyleix
Abbeyleix, Co. Laois. Tel: 0502-31450
Pleasant nine holes amid mature trees.

Achill Island
Achill, Co. Mayo. Tel: 098-43456
Quaint, open links in holiday setting by beach. Nine holes.

Adare
Adare Manor, Co. Limerick. Tel: 061-395044
Classic 18-hole parkland course designed by Robert Trent Jones, with
Victorian castle hotel as luxury amenity.

Adare Manor
Adare, Co. Limerick. Tel: 061-396204
18-hole parkland with historic castle as backdrop.

Antrim
c/o Allen Park Golf Centre, Castle Road, Antrim. Tel: 01849-429001
Three lakes form feature of 18-hole, gently undulating parkland.

Ardee
Ardee, Co. Louth. Tel: 041-53227
Parkland setting in trees with stream – 18 holes.

Ardfert
Tralee, Co. Kerry. Tel: 066-34744
Attractive nine-hole addition to Co. Kerry facilities.

Ardglass
Ardglass, Co. Down. Tel: 01396-841219
Hilly, 18-hole links running by seashore on Black Rock Cliffs.

Ardminnan
Portaferry, Co. Down. Tel: 012477-71321
18 holes in picturesque setting.

Arklow
Arklow, Co. Wicklow. Tel: 0402-32492
Unsung 18 holes of links quality.

Ashbourne
Ashbourne, Co. Meath. Tel: 01-8352005
Inviting, peaceful, 18-hole undulating parkland, encompassing
Broadmeadow River and lakes.

Ashfield
Cullyhanna, Co. Armagh. Tel: 01693-868180
18 holes bounded by Creggan River, with lake in play.

Ashford Castle
Cong, Co. Mayo. Tel: 092-46003
Lovely, undulating, nine-hole parkland course in five-star hotel grounds.

Athenry
Oranmore, Co. Galway. Tel: 091-794466
Successfully reconstructed to 18 holes in mature setting.

Athlone
Hodson Bay, Athlone, Co. Roscommon. Tel: 0902-92073
Much praised, 18-hole, parkland course in scenic river setting.

Athy
Geraldine, Athy, Co. Kildare. Tel: 0507-31729
Attractive, 18-hole, inland course.

Aughnacloy
Aughnacloy, Co. Tyrone. Tel: 016625-57050
Parkland nine holes of increasing repute.

Balbriggan
Blackhall, Balbriggan, Co. Dublin. Tel: 01-8412229
Fine parkland 18-holes, demonstrating dividends of loving care.

Balcarrick
Donabate, Co. Dublin. Tel: 01-8436957
18 holes of great variety and merit.

Ballaghaderreen
Aughalustia, Ballaghaderreen, Co. Roscommon. Tel: 0907-60295
Nine holes of toughening quality as trees mature.

Ballina
Shanaghy, Ballina, Co. Mayo. Tel: 096-21050
Fairly flat, 18-hole parkland.

Ballinamore
Ballinamore, Co. Leitrim. Tel: 078-44346
Tougher 18-hole test than first appears.

Ballinascorney
Tallaght, Co. Dublin. Tel: 01-4512516
Mixed challenge of flat and rising ground – 18 holes.

Above: *Adare Manor, Co. Limerick.*

Ballinasloe
Rossgloss, Ballinasloe, Co. Galway. Tel: 0905-42126
Good 18-hole course showing fruits of development programme.

Ballinrobe
Castlebar Road, Ballinrobe, Co. Mayo. Tel: 092-41118
18 holes partly set into racecourse.

Ballybofey and Stranorlar
Ballybofey, Co. Donegal. Tel: 074-31093
Popular, 18-hole parkland setting by lake.

Ballybunion (see page 12)

Ballycastle
Ballycastle, Co. Antrim. Tel: 012657-62536
18-hole mixed inland links overlooking shore, with views of Mull of Kintyre.

Ballyclare
Ballyclare, Co. Antrim. Tel: 019603-22696
Parkland course of 18 holes, designed by Peter Alliss.

Ballyhaunis
Coolnaha, Ballyhaunis, Co. Mayo. Tel: 0907-81398
Clever and varied nine-hole design.

Ballyheigue Castle
Ballyheigue, Tralee, Co. Kerry. Tel: 066-335555
Parkland nine holes, situated in scenic area.

Ballykisteen
Tipperary Town, Co. Tipperary. Tel: 062-33333
Wonderful Des Smyth-designed 18 holes, with attractive streams and lakes.

Ballyliffin
Clonmany, Co. Donegal. Tel: 077-76119
So nice that Nick Faldo wanted to buy it! Historic, seaside, 36-hole links complex of outstanding merit.

Ballymena
Broughshane, Ballymena, Co. Antrim. Tel: 01266-861487
Nice 18-hole course in rich parkland location.

Ballymote
Ballymote, Co. Sligo. Tel: 071-83158
Nine-hole parkland of substance.

Balmoral
Lisburn Road, Belfast. Tel: 01232-381514
Close to Belfast city, with clubhouse memorial to late Fred Daly – Ireland's only British Open champion. Tree lined, 18-hole course of merit.

Banbridge
Banbridge, Co. Down. Tel: 018206-62211
Inviting mix of easy walking and good views, successfully converted from 12 to 18 holes.

Bandon
Bandon, Co. Cork. Tel: 023-41111
Set in three parts, has testing, sloping contours – 18 holes.

Bangor
Broadsway, Bangor, Co. Down. Tel: 01247-270922
Long-established, top-quality, 18-hole championship course, set in rolling parkland.

Bantry Park
Donemark, Bantry, Co. Cork. Tel: 027-50579
Lovely 18 holes, enhanced by attractive setting.

Bearna
Corboley, Bearna, Galway. Tel: 091-592677
Exciting new 18 holes on typical Connemara moorland, commanding views of Galway Bay, Clare Hills and Aran Islands.

Beaufort
Killarney, Co. Kerry. Tel: 064-44440
On the foothills of Macgillycuddy Reeks, an Arthur Spring-18-hole creation of distinction.

Beaverstown
Bodenstown, Co. Dublin. Tel: 01-8436439
One-time commercial orchard, successfully converted – 18 holes.

Beech Park
Rathcoole, Co. Dublin. Tel: 01-4580522
Mature, 18-hole setting where condition belies newness of course.

Belturbet
Erne Hill, Belturbet, Co. Cavan. Tel: 049-22287
Nine holes with tough par three to finish.

Belvoir Park (see page 16)

Berehaven
Castletownbere, Bearhaven, Co. Cork. Tel: 027-70700
Fabulous setting by sea, with inlet running through most of nine holes.

Birr
Glenns, Birr, Co. Offaly. Tel: 0509-20082
Renowned for its mature, tree-lined location. Rolling 18 holes on good, sandy subsoil.

Black Bush
Dunshaughlin, Co. Meath. Tel: 01-8250021
27-hole complex with strong reputation.

Blacklion
Toam, Blacklion, Co. Cavan. Tel: 072-53024
18-hole inland variety.

Blackwood
Bangor, Co. Down. Tel: 01247-852706
Excellent pay-and-play complex in lovely setting, comprising par 71 and par 54 courses, plus driving range.

Blainroe
Blainroe, Co. Wicklow. Tel: 0404-68168
Quality, 18-hole parkland on undulating landscape overlooking Irish Sea.

Bodenstown
Sallins, Co. Kildare. Tel: 045-897096
Long but fair 18 well-varied holes. Also shorter 18-hole amenity.

Borris
Deerpark, Borris, Co. Carlow. Tel: 0503-73310
Exceptionally attractive nine-hole course in wooded surroundings.

Boyle
Knockadoodbrusna, Boyle, Co. Roscommon. Tel: 079-62192
Invigorating surroundings of mountain background – nine holes.

Bray
Ravenswell Road, Bray, Co. Wicklow. Tel: 01-2862484
Historic, well-varied, nine-hole, tree-lined course. Club has strong associations with beginning of golf in Ireland.

Bright Castle
Downpatrick, Co. Down. Tel: 01396-841319
Physically demanding, 18-hole, parkland course with five par fives.

Brown Trout
Aghadowny, Co. Derry. Tel: 01265-868209
Great character in wooded setting, with Agivey River in play. Nine holes.

Buncrana
Buncrana, Co. Donegal. Tel: 077-62279
Rugged nine-hole links.

Bundoran
Bundoran, Co. Donegal. Tel: 072-41302
One of Ireland's finest 18-hole, inland courses, partly on clifftop. Designed by Harry Vardon.

Bushfoot
Portballintrae, Co. Antrim. Tel: 012657-31317
Excellent, 18-hole links embracing River Bush.

Cabra Castle
Kingscourt, Co. Cavan. Tel: 042-67030
Pretty, parkland nine-holer.

Cahir Park
Kilcommon, Cahir, Co. Tipperary. Tel: 052-41474
Tilting 18 holes in classic park setting by River Suir.

Cairndhu
Larne, Co. Antrim. Tel: 01574-5833324
Built into hill, commands fabulous views. Testing, 18-hole parkland.

Callan
Callan, Co. Kilkenny. Tel: 056-25136
Well-distributed nine holes, toughened by stream.

Carlow (see page 20)

Carnalea
Bangor, Co. Down. Tel: 01247-270368
Seaside course with beautiful views. 18 holes.

Carne
Belmullet, Co. Mayo. Tel: 097-82292
Marvellous new links overlooking Blacksod Bay. Tremendous last six-hole climax, classically set amid the dunes.

Carrickfergus
Carrickfergus, Co. Antrim. Tel: 019603-63713
Terrifying first hole over large dam gives way to less testing, 18-hole, park layout.

Carrickmines
Carrickmines, Dublin 18. Tel: 01-2895676
Pretty nine holes set in hilly terrain.

Carrick-on-Shannon
Woodbrook, Carrick-on-Shannon, Co. Leitrim. Tel: 079-67015
Interesting blend of nine holes on part rising ground.

Carrick-on-Suir
Garravoone, Carrick-on-Suir, Co. Tipperary. Tel: 051-640558
Handsome 18 holes, in shadow of Comeragh Mountains.

Castle
Rathfarnham, Dublin 14. Tel: 01-4904207
One-time orchard, offering good 18 holes with rich variety.

Castlebar
Rocklands, Castlebar, Co. Mayo. Tel: 094-21649
Perfectly enjoyable, mature, 18-hole parkland.

Castle Barna
Daingean, Co. Offaly. Tel: 0506-53384
Partly alongside Grand Canal, 18-hole, rolling parkland.

Castleblayney
Onomy, Castleblayney, Co. Monaghan. Tel: 042-40451
Positioned between forest and lake on hilly terrain – nine holes.

Castlecomer
Castlecomer, Co. Kilkenny. Tel: 056-41139
Long in challenge and scenic in character. Outstanding nine holes.

Castlegregory
Stradbally, Castlegregory, Co. Kerry. Tel: 066-39444
Much acclaimed, nine-hole, traditional links, restored by designer Arthur Spring.

Castle Hume
Enniskillen, Co. Fermanagh. Tel: 01365-327077
18 holes, pleasant parkland running by lake shore.

Castlerea
Castlerea, Co. Roscommon. Tel: 0907-20203
River in play as extra highlight of nine holes amid trees.

Castlerock (see page 24)

Castletroy
Castletroy, Co. Limerick. Tel: 061-335753
Top-class, tree-lined, 18-hole parkland.

Castlewarden
Straffan, Co. Kildare. Tel: 01-4589254
Parkland course – 18 holes.

Ceann Sibéal (Dingle)
Ballyferriter, Co. Kerry. Tel: 066-56255
Links gem of 18 good holes with adjoining hotel.

Charlesland
Greystones, Co. Wicklow. Tel: 01-2876764
18 holes in nice seaside setting, with hotel facilities.

Charleville
Ardmore, Charleville, Co. Cork. Tel: 063-81257
Parkland course of 27 holes with lots of variety.

Christy O'Connor Centre
c/o Hollystown Golf Club, Mulhuddart, Dublin. Tel: 01-8207447
Very popular, 18-hole public facility, encompassing club named after legendary Irish professional.

Cill Dara
Little Curragh, Co. Kildare. Tel: 045-521443
Relatively undemanding 18-holer amidst colourful gorse.

City of Derry
Prehan, Co. Derry. Tel: 01504-46369
High-reputation, 18-hole parkland with water features.

City West
Saggart, Co. Dublin. Tel: 01-4588556
Attractive, visitor-friendly, 18-hole parkland with Macgregor golf academy/driving range and excellent hotel facilities.

Below: *Buncrana, Co. Donegal.*

Clandeboye
Newtownards, Co. Down. Tel: 01247-271767
Splendid Ava and Dufferin 18-hole heathland-parkland courses in complementary setting.

Claremorris
Castlemagarrett, Claremorris, Co. Mayo. Tel: 094-71572
Testing 18 holes with stream hazard.

Cliftonville
Westland Road, Belfast 14. Tel: 01232-746595
Unusual setting with nine holes built around waterworks on high ground.

Clones
Clones, Co. Monaghan. Tel: 047-56017
Richly varied nine holes in sylvan estate.

Clongowes Wood College
Naas, Co. Kildare. Tel: 045-868202
Private nine holes in school grounds.

Clonlara
Clonlara, Co. Clare. Tel: 061-354141
12-hole course in beautiful parkland by banks of River Shannon.

Clontarf
Donnycarney House, Malahide Road, Dublin 3. Tel: 01-8331892
Closest 18-hole course to Dublin city. Pleasant to play in tree-lined setting.

Cloughaneely
Falcarragh, Co. Donegal. Tel: 074-65416
Mature woodland location for pretty nine-hole challenge.

Cobh
Ballywilliam, Cobh, Co. Cork. Tel: 021-812399
Most pleasing nine-hole facility, in famous seaport.

Connemara (see page 28)

Connemara Isles
Lettermore, Connemara, Co. Galway. Tel: 091-572498
Ireland's only thatched clubhouse, with turf fires, provides unique 19th hole on island surrounding of rare beauty. Nine holes.

Coollattin
Shillelagh, Co. Wicklow. Tel: 055-29125
Classic parkland setting for good 18 holes.

Coosheen
Schull, Co. Cork. Tel: 028-28182
Six par threes in unusual nine holes atop scenic Schull Harbour.

Cork (see page 32)

Corrstown
St Margaret's, Co. Dublin. Tel: 01-8640533
27-hole parkland, well-stocked with trees.

County Armagh
Newry Road, Armagh. Tel: 01861-525861
Shortish, 18-hole, parkland course amid trees and with stream.

County Cavan
Drumellis, Co. Cavan. Tel: 049-31541
Parkland on some hilly ground – 18 holes.

County Longford
Glack, Co. Longford. Tel: 043-46310
Undulating, 18-hole parkland with prominent water features.

County Louth (see page 36)

County Sligo (see page 40)

County Tipperary
Dundrum, Co. Tipperary. Tel: 062-71116
Sited near historic Cashel, in rich pasturelands, on hotel grounds – 18 holes.

Courtown
Gorey, Co. Wexford. Tel: 055-25166
Popular, seaside 18 holes – 'inland' texture.

Craddockstown
Naas, Co. Kildare. Tel: 045-897610
Arthur Spring-designed 18 holes, containing decoratively linked lakes.

Crossgar
Downpatrick, Co. Down. Tel: 01396-831523
Not too testing nine holes.

Cruit Island
Kincasslagh, Co. Donegal. Tel: 075-43296
Nine-hole links course with winning appeal.

Curragh
Curragh Camp, Co. Kildare. Tel: 045-441714
Surprisingly hilly and long 18-hole course.

Curra West
Kylebrack, Loughrea, Co. Galway. Tel: 091-341318
Parkland nine holes.

Cushendall
Shore Road, Cushendall, Co. Antrim. Tel: 012667-71318
River Dall and 'out of bounds' predominant in tough nine-holer.

Deer Park
Deer Park Hotel, Howth, Co. Dublin. Tel: 01-8326093
Thriving, public 36-hole parkland facility of repute.

Delgany
Delgany, Co. Wicklow. Tel: 01-2874536
Some climbs with great holes and views as compensation – 18-hole parkland.

Delvin Castle
Delvin, Co. Westmeath. Tel: 044-64315
Lovely 18 holes of growing reputation in estate setting.

Djouce Mountain
Roundwood, Co. Wicklow. Tel: 01-2818585
Flat nine holes nestled in well-known beauty spot between Dublin and Wicklow Mountains.

Donabate
Donabate, Co. Dublin. Tel: 01-8436346
Undulating, 18-hole parkland with handsome foliage.

Donaghadee
Warren Road, Donaghadee, Co. Down. Tel: 01247-883624
Welcoming, holiday, 18-hole parkland, with views to Isle of Man and beyond.

Donegal (see page 44)

Doneraile
Doneraile, Co. Cork. Tel: 022-24137
Highly regarded parkland nine-holer.

Dooks
Glenbeigh, Co. Kerry. Tel: 066-68205
Fine linksland 18 holes, rich in character and tradition.

Douglas
Douglas, Co. Cork. Tel: 021-895297
High-class, 18-hole, parkland challenge worthy of reputation.

Downpatrick
Saul Road, Downpatrick, Co. Down. Tel: 01396-615947
Typical parkland 18 holes, boosted by scenic value.

Down Royal
Maze, Lisburn, Co. Antrim. Tel: 01846-621339
18 holes within more famous Down Royal Racecourse.

Dromoland Castle
Newmarket-on-Fergus, Co. Clare. Tel: 061-368444
Set in rich, rolling estate in five-star hotel grounds. 18 inviting holes.

Druids Glen (see page 48)

Dublin and County
Corballis, Donabate, Co. Dublin. Tel: 01-8436228
Well-maintained, 18-hole, public course.

Dublin Mountain
Brittas, Co. Dublin. Tel: 01-4582622
Parkland 18 holes, visitors welcomed.

Dundalk
Blackrock, Dundalk, Co. Louth. Tel: 042-21731
18-hole parkland, reaping dividends of refurbishment programme.

Dunfanaghy
Dunfanaghy, Co. Donegal. Tel: 074-36335
Pleasant, 18-hole links, sited on exposed point towards Horn Head.

Dungannon
Dungannon, Co. Tyrone. Tel: 01868-727338
18 holes in rich pastureland spiced with some great holes.

Dungarvan
Ballinacourty, Dungarvan, Co. Waterford. Tel: 058-41605
Tough finishing stretch along sea to well-blended 18 holes.

Dun Laoghaire
Tivoli Road, Dun Laoghaire, Co. Dublin. Tel: 01-2803916
18-hole, suburban parkland with plentiful par threes.

Dunmore
Clonakilty, Co. Cork. Tel: 023-33858
Nine holes, demanding accuracy from tees.

Dunmore East
Dunmore East, Co. Waterford. Tel: 051-383151
Hill-top setting overlooking attractive tourist fishing village – 18-hole parkland.

Dunmurry
Dunmurry, Co. Antrim. Tel: 01232-610834
Improved excellently in short lifespan – 18-hole parkland.

East Clare
Scarriff, Co. Clare. Tel: 061-921322
Settling 18 holes on renowned tourist route.

East Cork
Midleton, Co. Cork. Tel: 021-631687
Tight, tree-lined, 18-hole parkland.

Edenderry
Edenderry, Co. Offaly. Tel: 0405-31072
Built on bog-peat, 18 holes of attractive mix.

Edenmore
Magheralin, Co. Antrim. Tel: 01846-611310
Inviting, open and undulating, 18-hole parkland.

Edmondstown
Rathfarnham, Dublin 14. Tel: 01-4931082
18-hole parkland, improved upon following development.

Elmgreen
Castleknock, Dublin 15. Tel: 01-8200797
Well-run, pay-and-play 18 holes in lovely setting, also encompassing pitch and putt course and driving range.

Elm Park
Nutley Lane, Donnybrook, Dublin 4. Tel: 01-2693438
Most satisfying 18 holes of mature and wooded parkland with feature stream.

Ennis
Drumbiggle, Ennis, Co. Clare. Tel: 065-24074
Undulating, 18-hole parkland of fine standing. Noted for fast, sloping greens.

Enniscorthy
Knockmarshal, Enniscorthy, Co. Wexford. Tel: 054-33191
Purchase of additional prime land has brought rich rewards – 18 holes.

Enniscrone
Enniscrone, Co. Sligo. Tel: 096-36297
Fine, championship, 18-hole links of deserving repute.

Enniskillen
Enniskillen, Co. Fermanagh. Tel: 01365-325250
Parkland setting with 18 holes.

Esker Hills
Tullamore, Co. Offaly. Tel: 0506-55999
Quality 18 holes in attractive hilly parkland.

European Club, The (see page 50)

Fermoy
Fermoy, Co. Cork. Tel: 025-32694
18-hole inland with distinct undulation.

Fernhill
Carrigaline, Co. Cork. Tel: 021-373103
Pleasant, 18-hole parkland.

Finnstown
Finnstown House Hotel, Lucan, Co. Dublin. Tel: 01-6280644
Enjoyable, nine-hole, luxury hotel amenity, designed by Christy O'Connor Snr.

Fintona
Fintona, Co. Tyrone. Tel: 01662-841480
Appealing, nine-hole, parkland layout, with added fishing facility.

Forrest Little
Cloghran, Co. Dublin. Tel: 01-8401763
Matured, 18-hole parkland, next door to Dublin Airport.

Fortwilliam
Downview Avenue, Belfast. Tel: 01232-370770
Hilly, 18-hole parkland.

Fota Island (see page 52)

Four Lakes
Sallins, Co. Kildare. Tel: 045-66003
Watch out for water on this maturing, 18-hole parkland.

Foxrock
Torquay Road, Foxrock, Dublin 18. Tel: 01-2893992
Satisfying nine holes in nice wooded setting.

Foyle
Alder Road, Derry. Tel: 01504-352222
Excellent new all-purpose centre, with 18-hole championship layout, driving range and short course.

Frankfield
Douglas, Co. Cork. Tel: 021-361199
Sited on hill overlooking Cork city, nine holes with golf range.

Galgorm Castle
Ballymena, Co. Antrim. Tel: 01266-650210
Outstanding 18 holes in grounds of distinctive Galgorm Castle, featuring river and lake.

Galway
Salthill, Galway. Tel: 091-522033
Situated by Galway Bay – 18 holes colourfully set amidst gorse and shrubbery.

Galway Bay
Renvyle Road, Roanmore, Galway. Tel: 091-790500
Christy O'Connor Jnr., 18-hole design set into Galway Bay, with quality hotel facilities.

Gilnahirk
Braniel Road, Gilnahirk, Belfast. Tel: 01232-448477
Hilly nine holes, with no par five!

Glasson
Athlone, Co. Westmeath. Tel: 0902-85120
Scenic, 18-hole parkland on shores of Lough Ree.

Glengarriff
Glengarriff, Co. Cork. Tel: 027-63150
Outstandingly beautiful setting by Bantry Bay. Nine-hole parkland.

Glenmalure
Rathdrum, Co. Wicklow. Tel: 0404-46679
Delightful 18 holes in picturesque Vale of Avoca.

Glen of the Downs
Glen of the Downs, Co. Wicklow. Tel: 01-2864585
Challenging, new, 18-hole parkland in scenic splendour.

Gold Coast
Dungarvan, Co. Waterford. Tel: 058-44055
Lovely parkland setting, with plans to extend to 18 holes.

Gormanston College
Franciscan College, Gormanston, Co. Meath. Tel: 01-8412203
Private nine holes in school grounds.

Gort
Gort, Co. Galway. Tel: 091-632244
Upgraded to 18 holes while retaining all its best characteristics – scenery and out of bounds!

Gracehill
Stranocum, Ballymoney, Co. Antrim. Tel: 01265-751209
Tough, nine-hole challenge, dominated by water hazards.

Grange (see page 54)

Grange Castle
Nangor Road, Clondalkin, Dublin 22. Tel: 01-4641043
Championship quality, pay-and-play 18 holes, encompassing four lakes which affect nine holes.

Green Acres
Ballyclare, Co. Antrim. Tel: 01960-354111
Rural-set 18 holes of true merit, with driving range.

Greencastle
Greencastle, via Lifford, Co. Donegal. Tel: 077-81013
Challenging nine holes, hard by shores of Inishowen Peninsula.

Green Island
Green Island, Co. Antrim. Tel: 01232-862236
Scenic nine-holer with streams in play.

Greenore
Greenore, Co. Louth. Tel: 042-73678
Interesting blend of links and parkland texture. Good-quality 18 holes.

Greystones
Greystones, Co. Wicklow. Tel: 01-2874136
Popular, 18-hole parkland, enhanced by new holes and clubhouse.

Gweedore
Derrybeg, Letterkenny, Co. Donegal. Tel: 075-31140
Perfectly enjoyable 18 holes, with some running by seashore.

Harbour Point
Little Island, Cork. Tel: 021-354544
Spectacular 18-hole parkland development, by architectural hand of Paddy Merrigan.

Hazel Grove
Jobstown, Tallaght, Dublin 24. Tel: 01-4520911
Elevated nine-hole parkland overlooking Dublin city.

Headfort
Kells, Co. Meath. Tel: 046-40146
Classic, 18-hole parkland in lovely countryside.

Heath
The Heath, Portlaoise, Co. Laoise. Tel: 0502-46533
Long-established, though unsung, 18 holes amidst gorse.

Helen's Bay
Golf Road, Bangor, Co. Down. Tel: 01247-852815
Seaside nine holes of good variety.

Hermitage (see page 58)

Highfield
Carbury, Co. Kildare. Tel: 0405-31021
Family-run 18 holes on flat terrain, amidst attractive variety of trees.

Hibernian (see City West)

Hollywood Lakes
Ballyboughal, Co. Dublin. Tel: 01-8433407
Long course, containing 639-yard 14th hole and much water!

Holywood
Demesne Road, Holywood, Co. Down. Tel: 01232-423135
Physically demanding, 18-hole parkland.

Above: *Howth, Dublin.*

Howth
Sutton, Dublin 13. Tel: 01-8323055
Notably hilly 18 holes on heathland turf, commanding panoramic views of Dublin city and bay.

Island (see page 62)

Kanturk
Fairy Hill, Kanturk, Co. Cork. Tel: 029-50534
18 holes amidst mature plantation, with premium on accuracy.

Kenmare
Kenmare, Co. Kerry. Tel: 064-41291
Largely a holiday 18-holer, amidst trees and colourful shrubbery. Superb scenery.

Kerries
Tralee, Co. Kerry. Tel: 066-22112
Beautiful parkland nine holes, overlooking lovely Tralee Bay and Dingle Peninsula.

Kilcock
Gallow, Kilcock, Co. Meath. Tel: 01-6284074
Extended to 18 holes of welcoming variety. Stream in play at four holes.

Kilcoole
Newcastle Road, Co. Wicklow. Tel: 01-2872066
Handsomely redeveloped 9 holes, with telling water features.

Kildare (see page 66)

Kilkee
East End, Kilkee, Co. Clare. Tel: 065-56048
Commands tremendous views over Atlantic cliff. 18 holes.

Kilkenny
Glendine, Kilkenny city. Tel: 056-65400
Rolling 18-hole parkland course of great respect.

Killarney (see page 70)

Killeen
Kill, Co. Kildare. Tel: 045-866003
Cleverly designed, top-quality 18 holes.

Killeline
Newcastle West, Co. Limerick. Tel: 069-61600
18 holes amidst major tree plantation.

Killinbeg
Dundalk, Co. Louth. Tel: 042-39303
Nice, 18-hole parkland, in shadow of Killin Wood and with river in play.

Killiney
Ballinclea Road, Killiney, Co. Dublin. Tel: 01-2852823
One of Dublin's most scenically set, hillside, nine-hole parkland layouts.

Killorglin
Steal Roe, Killorglin, Co. Kerry. Tel: 066-61979
Relatively new 18 holes, with growing reputation, in renowned golf/tourism location.

Killymoon
Cookstown, Co. Tyrone. Tel: 016487-63762
Parkland, 18-hole course with six par threes!

Kilrea
Kilrea, Co. Derry. Tel: 01266-71397
Tranquil, heathland nine holes, with three par threes running consecutively.

Kilrush
Kilrush, Co. Clare. Tel: 065-51138
Profiting from constant refurbishment. 18 holes of additional scenic virtue.

Kilternan
Enniskerry Road, Kilternan, Co. Dublin. Tel: 01-2955559
Challenging, hillside, 18-hole parkland, encircling hotel with ski practice facilities.

Kinsale (New)
Farrangalway, Kinsale, Co. Cork. Tel: 021-774722
Additional 18-hole amenity with water features, in popular tourist destination.

Kinsale (Old)
Kinsale, Co. Cork. Tel: 021-772197
Blissful nine holes on hillside overlooking famous harbour.

Kirkistown Castle
Cloughey, Newtownards, Co. Down. Tel: 01247-71233
18-hole links quality, toughened by sea winds.

Knock
Newtownards Road, Belfast. Tel: 01232-483251
Typical 18-hole parkland suburban course, with river crossing many holes.

Knockanally
Donadea, Co. Kildare. Tel: 045-869322
Some excellent holes abound in mature, 18-hole layout amidst much timber.

Knockbracken
Knockbracken, Co. Down. Tel: 01232-401811
18-hole parkland, centrepiece of multisports complex.

Lahinch (see page 76)

Lambeg
Lisburn, Co. Antrim. Tel: 01846-662738
Short, municipal 18 holes, no par five, six par threes.

Larne
Island Magee, Co. Antrim. Tel: 01960-382228
Nine holes, mixed parkland/links.

Laytown and Bettystown
Bettystown, Co. Meath. Tel: 041-27170
Deceptively tough 18-hole links.

Lee Valley
Ovens, Co. Cork. Tel: 021-331721
Rural, wooded setting for delightful 18 holes with driving range.

Leixlip
Leixlip, Co. Kildare. Tel: 01-6244978
Nine-hole parkland in pretty setting.

Letterkenny
Letterkenny, Co. Donegal. Tel: 074-21150
Tough, 18-hole parkland with demanding finish.

Limerick
Ballyclough, Limerick. Tel: 061-415146
Much-praised, 18-hole parkland, amidst plentiful trees.

Limerick County
Ballyneety, Co. Limerick. Tel: 061-351881
Des Smyth-designed 18 holes, plus driving range and holiday home amenity.

Lisburn
Lisburn, Co. Antrim. Tel: 01846-677216
18-hole parkland commanding nice views over Lagan Valley.

Lismore
Lismore, Co. Waterford. Tel: 058-54026
Undulating nine holes in Lismore Castle grounds.

Above: *Luttrellstown Castle, Co. Dublin.*

Loughrea
Craigu, Loughrea, Co. Galway. Tel: 091-841049
Premium on approach shots. 18-hole parkland.

Lucan
Celbridge Road, Lucan, Co. Dublin. Tel: 01-6282106
Double par five finish to strong 18-hole parkland.

Lurgan
The Demesne, Lurgan, Co. Antrim. Tel: 01762-322087
Tough, 18-hole parkland, demanding accuracy.

Luttrellstown Castle
Clonsilla, Co. Dublin. Tel: 01-8089988
Much acclaimed, 18-hole, parkland course of distinction.

Macroom
Luckaduve, Macroom, Co. Cork. Tel: 026-41072
Parkland, undulating 18 holes with river as added feature.

Mahee Island
Newtownards, Co. Down. Tel: 01238-541234
Beautifully set in Strangford Lough, an undulating and exacting nine holes.

Mahon
Blackrock, Co. Cork. Tel: 021-252212
Successful, 18-hole public facility, built on marvellous location by river bank.

Malahide
Beechwood, The Grange, Malahide, Co. Dublin. Tel: 01-8461611
27-hole complex with fascinating variety and streams in play.

Mallow
Ballyellis, Mallow, Co. Cork. Tel: 022-21145
Invigorating, 18-hole, rolling parkland, finishing with a feature par three.

Malone (see page 82)

Mannin Castle
Carrickmacross, Co. Monaghan. Tel: 042-61714
Hospitable nine-hole parkland. Visitors welcome.

Massereene
Lough Road, Antrim. Tel: 01849-428096
Noted for its dry, sandy soil with Lough Neagh an adjacent attraction.

Milltown
Lr. Churchtown Road, Milltown, Dublin 14. Tel: 01-4976090
Appealing, centrally located, 18-hole parkland.

Mitchelstown
Mitchelstown, Co. Cork. Tel: 025-24072
18-hole parkland in charming setting near Galtee Mountains.

Moate
Moate, Co. Westmeath. Tel: 0902-81270
18-hole parkland, notably narrow in places.

Monkstown
Monkstown, Co. Cork. Tel: 021-841376
Challenging, 18-hole, heavily tree-lined parkland, with views of Lee Estuary.

Mountbellew
Mountbellew, Ballinasloe, Co. Galway. Tel: 0905-79259
Parkland course of nine holes with plenty of shot-making variety.

Mount Juliet (see page 86)

Mount Ober
Ballymaconaghy Road, Belfast. Tel: 01232-401811
18-hole, parkland course, driving range and practice ski facilities in excellent complex.

Mountrath
Knockinina, Mountrath, Co. Laois. Tel: 0502-32558
Fairly tight and lush, upgraded, 18-hole parkland.

Mount Temple
Moate, Co. Westmeath. Tel: 0902-81545
Part links/parkland, 18 holes with water features.

Mount Wolseley
Tullow, Co. Carlow. Tel: 0503-51674
On estate of Wolseley car family. Destined to mature into 18-hole parkland of true merit, with quality hotel facilities.

Mourne
Newcastle, Co. Down. Tel: 013967-23889
Welcoming 'little brother' nestled beside more formidable Royal Co. Down links.

Moyola Park
Castledawson, Magherafelt, Co. Derry. Tel: 01648-68468
Moyolla River bisects 18-hole parkland set among trees.

Mullingar (see page 90)

Mulrany
Mulrany, Westport, Co. Mayo. Tel: 098-36262
Nine-hole links in lovely setting by Clew Bay.

Muskerry
Carrigrohane, Co. Cork. Tel: 021-385297
Distinctly steep in places. 18-hole parkland with river feature.

Naas
Kerdiffstown, Naas, Co. Kildare. Tel: 045-874644
Popular, 18-hole parkland of much virtue.

Nairn and Portnoo
Nairn, Portnoo, Co. Donegal. Tel: 075-45107
Another unsung, scenic, Donegal gem, largely links – 18 holes.

Nenagh
Nenagh, Co. Tipperary. Tel: 067-34808
Quality, 18-hole parkland, favourably considered.

Newcastle West
Ardagh Village, Newcastle West, Co. Limerick. Tel: 069-76500
Settling new siting for long-established club. 18 holes with bonus of practice range.

Newlands
Clondalkin, Dublin 22. Tel: 01-4593157
Challenging, 18-hole, tree-lined course, originally laid out by legendary James Braid.

New Ross
Tinneranny, New Ross, Co. Wexford. Tel: 051-412433
Accuracy a premium on compact, 18-hole parkland.

Newtownstewart
Newtownstewart, Omagh, Co. Tyrone. Tel: 016626-61466
Picturesque and much frequented 18-hole parkland.

North West
Lisfannon, Fahan, Co. Donegal. Tel: 077-61027
Another of Co. Donegal's links treasures – 18 holes.

Nuremore
Nuremore, Carrickmacross, Co. Monaghan. Tel: 042-61438
Undulating, 18-hole parkland in hotel grounds, with strong water highlights.

Old Conna
Ferndale Road, Bray, Co. Wicklow. Tel: 01-2826055
Scenically set, 18-hole, parkland course of maturing quality.

Old Head
Kinsale, Co. Cork. Tel: 021-778444
Unique 18 holes laid out on historic clifftop, adjacent to ancient Kinsale harbour. Wondrous holes and breathtaking views.

Omagh
Dublin Road, Omagh, Co. Tyrone. Tel: 01662-241442
Hilly, 18-hole parkland, commanding lovely scenery.

Open Golf Centre
St Margaret's, Co. Dublin. Tel: 01-8640324
Flat, pay-and-play public concept, with driving range facility – 18 holes.

Ormeau
Ravenhill Road, Belfast. Tel: 01232-640700
Tranquil, nine-hole parkland, in close proximity to Belfast city centre.

Otway
Rathmullan, Letterkenny, Co. Donegal. Tel: 074-58319
Short, criss-crossing, hilly nine-holer.

Oughterard
Oughterard, Co. Galway. Tel: 091-552131
18-hole parkland, deriving benefits of good landscaping.

Parknasilla
Sneem, Co. Kerry. Tel: 064-45122
Excellent, nine-hole added facility, in beautiful grounds of Great Southern Hotel.

Portadown
Gilford Road, Portadown, Co. Armagh. Tel: 01762-355356
Attractively laid out, 18-hole parkland, with River Bann in play.

Portarlington
Garryhinch, Portarlington, Co. Laois. Tel: 0502-23044
Solid 18 holes amidst plentiful foliage, with water features.

Portmarnock (see page 94)

Portmarnock Hotel (see page 100)

Portsalon
Portsalon, Letterkenny, Co. Donegal. Tel: 074-59459
Long-established, traditional, 18-hole links course, well worth visiting.

Portstewart (see page 102)

Portumna
Portumna, Co. Galway. Tel: 0509-41059
18 holes, quietly laid out in forest park, with classic par-three finish.

Powerscourt
Powerscourt Estate, Enniskerry, Co. Wicklow. Tel: 01-2760503
Outstanding, 18-hole, championship status, parkland course in famous estate, commanding stunning views.

Rafeen Creek
Ringaskiddy, Co. Cork. Tel: 021-378430
Marvellous nine holes of variety, most especially tee shots over water at eighth and ninth.

Rathdowney
Rathdowney, Co. Laois. Tel: 0505-46107
Now developed to full 18-hole parkland, offering good variety.

Below: *Powerscourt, Co. Wicklow.*

Rathfarnham
Newtown, Rathfarnham, Dublin 16. Tel: 01-4931561
John Jacobs designed these undulating nine holes with commanding views.

Rathmore
Portrush, Co. Antrim. Tel: 01265-822996
Lesser known nine-hole links 'sister' of more esteemed Royal Portrush.

Rathsallagh
Dunlavin, Co. Wicklow. Tel: 045-403316
Luxury, family-owned, 18-hole parkland, surrounding manor house hotel.

Redcastle
Moville, Co. Donegal. Tel: 077-82073
Inviting nine holes by Lough Foyle, with added facility of hotel on site.

Ringdufferin
Toye, Killyleagh, Co. Down. Tel: 01396-828812
Ambitious plans to extend to 18 holes, overlooking shores of Strangford Lough.

Ring of Kerry
Templenoe, Kenmare, Co. Kerry. Tel: 064-42000
Beautifully set 18-hole parkland, designed by Roger Jones.

Rockmount
Carryduff, Belfast. Tel: 01232-812279
Recommended 18-hole parkland, in peaceful rural ambience, with views of Mountains of Mourne.

Rockwell College
Cashel, Co. Tipperary. Tel: 062-61444
Private nine holes in school grounds.

Roe Park
Limavady, Co. Derry. Tel: 015047-60105
Frequent water challenges on quality, 18-hole parkland course, enjoying marvellous scenery.

Rosapenna
Downings, Co. Donegal. Tel: 074-55301
Historic, 18-hole links/inland mix, tracing its architecture to Old Tom Morris, James Braid and Harry Vardon. Visitor-friendly, on-site hotel a popular destination.

Roscommon
Moate Park, Roscommon. Tel: 0903-26382
Tough, 18-hole parkland.

Roscrea
Derryvale, Roscrea, Co. Tipperary. Tel: 0505-21130
Five par threes provide feature of popular, 18-hole parkland.

Ross
Killarney, Co. Kerry. Tel: 064-31125
A nine-hole gem to enhance further Killarney's golfing reputation.

Rosslare
Rosslare Strand, Co. Wexford.
Very popular, 27-hole, links complex along seashore.

Rossmore
Rossmore Park, Monaghan. Tel: 047-81316
Water hazards a feature of 18-hole, parkland layout.

Roundwood
Newtownmountkennedy, Co. Wicklow. Tel: 01-2818488
Constructed to the highest standards in wooded area popular with tourists. Enjoying stunning vista. 18 holes.

Royal Belfast (see page 106)

Above: *Slieve Russell, Co. Cavan.*

Royal Co. Down (see page 112)

Royal Dublin (see page 116)

Royal Portrush (see page 120)

Royal Tara
Bellinter, Navan, Co. Meath. Tel: 046-25508
Lovely, 18-hole, parkland setting, designed by Des Smyth.

Rush
Rush, Co. Dublin. Tel: 01-8438177
Quaint and excellent nine-hole links.

St Annes
North Bull Island, Dollymount, Dublin 5. Tel: 01-8336471
Links quality 18 holes.

St Helen's Bay
St Helen's, Kilrane, Co. Wexford. Tel: 053-33234
Philip Walton-designed 18 holes on clifftop setting, with cottage accommodation on site.

St Margaret's
Dublin Airport, Co. Dublin. Tel: 01-8640400
Spectacular, 18-hole parkland with water hazard feature.

Scrabo
Scrabo Road, Newtownards, Co. Down. Tel: 01247-812355
Strenuous but scenic 18 holes, with panoramic mountain and sea views.

Seapoint
Termonfeckin, Co. Louth. Tel: 041-22333
Relatively new 18-hole links of merit.

Shandon Park
Shandon Park, Belfast. Tel: 01232-401856
Parkland course of 18-holes, championship standard, with well-earned reputation.

Shannon
Shannon Airport, Co. Clare. Tel: 061-471849
Long, 18-hole parkland, beside Shannon Airport.

Silverwood
Lurgan, Co. Armagh. Tel: 01762-326606
Popular 18-hole development, with attractive stream features.

Skerries
Hacketstown, Skerries, Co. Dublin. Tel: 01-8491567
Enhanced reputation as a consequence of course and clubhouse development. 18-hole parkland.

Skibbereen
Licknavar, Skibbereen, Co. Cork. Tel: 028-21227
Pleasant, 18-hole parkland.

Slade Valley
Brittas, Co. Dublin. Tel: 01-4582739
Strong on scenery – 18-hole parkland.

Slieve Russell
Ballyconnell, Co. Cavan. Tel: 049-26444
Excellent new 18-hole creation in luxury hotel grounds.

Spa
Ballinahinch, Co. Down. Tel: 01238-562365
Tight, 18-hole, parkland course with good views of mountains.

Spanish Point
Milltown Malbay, Co. Clare. Tel: 065-84198
Classic linksland with unique sequence of six par threes and three par fours!

Stackstown
Rathfarnham, Dublin 16. Tel: 01-4941993
Fabulous clubhouse setting overlooking Dublin – 18 holes in hilly parkland.

Stepaside
Stepaside, Co. Dublin. Tel: 01-2952859
Nine-hole, pay-and-play, mature parkland.

Strabane
Ballycolman, Strabane, Co. Tyrone. Tel: 01504-382007
18-hole parkland at foot of Sperrin Mountains, combining good scenery with strong golfing virtue.

Strandhill
Strandhill, Co. Sligo. Tel: 071-68188
Top-class, popular, 18-hole links.

Strokestown
Strokestown, Co. Roscommon. Tel: 078-33100
Inviting nine holes in sylvan setting overlooking lakes.

Sutton
Cush Point, Sutton, Co. Dublin. Tel: 01-8322965
Tight nine holes by seaside, synonymous with legendary Joe Carr.

Swinford
Brabazon Park, Swinford, Co. Mayo. Tel: 094-51378
Nice, tree-lined nine-hole course.

Swords
Swords, Co. Dublin. Tel: 01-8409819
Worthy 18-hole parkland, visitors welcome.

Tandragee
Markethill Road, Tandragee, Co. Armagh. Tel: 01782-841272
Mature, 18-hole, parkland course with nice views towards Mourne Mountains.

Tara Glen
Ballymoney, Gorey, Co. Wexford. Tel: 055-25413
Popular, seaside nine holes, in holiday location.

Temple
Boardmills, Lisburn, Co. Antrim. Tel: 01846-639213
Nine holes with double tees and panoramic mountain views.

Templemore
Templemore, Co. Tipperary. Tel: 0504-31522
Compact nine-hole parkland.

Thurles
Turtulla, Thurles, Co. Tipperary. Tel: 0504-24599
Classic 18-hole parkland with style and character.

Tipperary
Rathanny, Tipperary, Co. Tipperary. Tel: 062-51119
Once had no bunkers, now handsomely updated and extended to 18 holes.

Townley Hall
Tullyallen, Drogheda, Co. Louth. Tel: 041-42229
Parkland nine holes. Visitors always welcome.

Tralee (see page 126)

Tramore (see page 130)

Trim
Newtownmoynagh, Trim, Co. Meath. Tel: 046-31463
Much-loved, 18-hole, parkland layout.

Tuam
Barnacurragh, Tuam, Co. Galway. Tel: 093-28993
Parkland setting, greatly upgraded – 18 holes.

Tubbercurry
Tubbercurry, Co. Sligo. Tel: 071-85849
Old club revived on new, nine-hole, parkland site.

Tulfarris
Blessington, Co. Wicklow.
18 holes in tree-lined, pretty setting, with on-site hotel.

Tullamore (see page 134)

Turvey
Donabate, Co. Dublin. Tel: 01-8435169
18 holes in nice parkland.

Virginia
Virginia, Co. Cavan. Tel: 049-48066
Nine-hole parkland in appealing hotel setting.

Warrenpoint
Lr. Dromore Road, Warrenpoint, Co. Down. Tel: 01693-753695
Scenic and mature, tree-sheltered, 18-hole parkland which produced Walker-Ryder Cup star Ronan Rafferty.

Waterford
Newrath, Waterford. Tel: 051-876748
Popular, 18-hole, mature parkland on tilting terrain with good views.

Waterford Castle
The Island, Waterford. Tel: 051-871633
Spectacular, 18-hole, island parkland, created by Des Smyth, with luxury hotel.

Waterville (see page 138)

Westmanstown
Clonsilla, Dublin 15. Tel: 01-8205817
Maturing, flat, 18-hole development, part of Garda Siochana sports complex.

Westport (see page 142)

West Waterford
Dungarvan, Co. Waterford. Tel: 058-43216
Rolling parkland on banks of Brickey River. Eddie Hackett-designed 18 holes.

Wexford
Mulgannon, Co. Wexford. Tel: 053-42238
Commands lovely views to augment value of well-matured, 18-hole parkland.

Whitehead
Carrickfergus, Co. Antrim. Tel: 01960-353631
Good seaside/parkland 18-hole mix, with fabulous sea views.

Wicklow
Dunbur Road, Wicklow. Tel: 0404-67379
Rare clifftop setting – a nine-hole beauty.

Woodbrook (see page 146)

Woodenbridge
Woodenbridge, Arklow, Co. Wicklow. Tel: 0402-35202
Breathtaking ambience in renowned vale alongside Avoca River. Outstanding 18 holes amidst trees and river.

Woodlands
Coolereagh, Coill Dubh, Co. Kildare. Tel: 045-860777
Nine-hole parkland with ambitions to blossom to full 18.

Woodstock
Ennis, Co. Clare. Tel: 065-29463
Unusual for fact that 18 holes are laid out on three levels, with river and lakes as added highlights.

Youghal
Knockaverry, Youghal, Co. Cork. Tel: 024-92787
Hilltop, 18-hole test, with good dog-leg variety and superb sea views, beside ancient and distinctive town.